Notions of
Beauty & Sexuality
in Black Communities
IN THE CARIBBEAN AND BEYOND

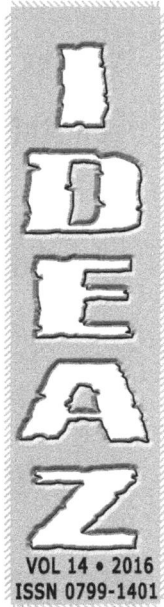

IDEAZ

VOL 14 • 2016
ISSN 0799-1401

GUEST EDITORS

Michael Barnett *and* Clinton Hutton

ARAWAK
publications
KINGSTON · JAMAICA

RESOURCE *Publications* · Eugene, Oregon

Notions of Beauty & Sexuality in Black Communities in the Caribbean and Beyond

GUEST EDITORS
Michael Barnett *and* Clinton Hutton

IDEAZ

Editor Ian Boxill

Vol. 14 • 2016

ISSN 0799-1401

Ideaz-Institute for Intercultural and Comparative Research /
Ideaz-Institut für interkulturelle und vergleichende Forschung
Contact and Publisher: **www.ideaz-institute.com**

IDEAZ-Journal
Publisher: Arawak publications • Kingston, Jamaica

Credits
 Cover photo –Courtesy of
  Lance Watson, photographer & *Chyna Whyne*, model
 Photos reproduced in text –Courtesy of
  Clinton Hutton (Figs. 2.1, 4.4, 4.5, G-1, G-2, G-5)
  David Barnett (Fig. 4.1)
  MITS, UWI (Figs. 4.2, 4.3)
  Lance Watson (Figs. 4.6, 4.7, G.3, G-4)
  Annie Paul (Figs. 6.1, 6.2, 6.3)
  Benjamin Asomoah (Figs. G-6, G-7)

Printed and distributed in North America by Resource Publications, an
imprint of Wipf and Stock Publishers, 199 West 8th Avenue, Ste 3, Eugene,
OR 97401. All rights reserved.

ISBN: 978-1-5326-1405-7

CONTENTS

Figure G-1 • Natchana Phipps

EDITORIAL

Michael Barnett & Clinton Hutton
- Guest Editors -

Welcome to this special issue of IDEAZ which focuses on notions of beauty and sexuality among black women in black communities in the Caribbean, the African Diaspora and beyond. The articles presented here touch on a subject area that is often considered as merely personal, but in reality is one that is very political. Notions of beauty and sexuality that exist in black communities in truth speak to the matter of identity politics – a phenomenon of great sociological, psychological and cultural significance for any society, nation, or group of people. In our opinion it is an area that warrants more attention, consideration, and introspection if meaningful human development is to take place – certainly as far as the Caribbean region is concerned. In fact we would go so far as to say that in societies where groups of people are fundamentally uncomfortable with their natural self-image, there will be impediments to meaningful development and progress for such groups and the societies they comprise.

This special issue was inspired by a series of Black History month forums on notions of beauty in black communities, conceptualized by Michael Barnett and programmed by the Department of Sociology, Psychology and Social Work, The University of the West Indies (UWI), Mona and launched February 2012.

The array of articles in this journal sucessfully explores and interrogates how notions of beauty and sexuality within Black communities are influenced by racialized and gendered social constructions of difference.

The first article in this volume, written by Imani Tafari-Ama, a scholar who specializes in gender and development studies as well as Rastafari studies, considers the practices of skin bleaching and hair straightening among black women in general, She argues that these practices are indicators of internalized racism and the reproduction of dominant (hegemonic) ideals of beauty. She goes further to label these practices as part of a psychosis that has afflicted members of the African Diaspora resulting from a phenomenon labelled "post-traumatic slavery syndrome", described in detail by Joy DeGruy

IDEAZ Vol. 14 • 2016 • ISSN 0799-1401
© Centre for Tourism & Policy Research / Ian Boxill – UWI, Mona

Leary (2005).

The second article, written by political scientist and philosopher Clinton Hutton, examines the definition, construction and cultivation of the ontology of white supremacy and the considerable influence that it has had globally. It also examines how Africans in the Americas counteracted or embraced the white aesthetic construction of Blackness.

The third article, written by anthropology professor Jean Rahier, examines issues of beauty and sexuality in regard to Black women in Ecuador. It first considers the persistently held stereotyped perceptions of Black women in Ecuador as hyper-sexualized beings; and then how Ecuadorian Black women perceive themselves in terms of the dynamics of beauty and sexuality, on a case study basis.

Next, sociology lecturer Michael Barnett considers the factors that influence African Caribbean women, and women in the Americas in general, to alter their natural hair, either chemically or otherwise. Additionally, this article considers why some women of African descent choose to wear their hair with its natural texture.

Anthropology lecturer Doreen Gordon considers the comparative meanings of beauty among upwardly mobile Black people in Brazil and Jamaica. In this fifth article, the main argument is that consumption around beauty is one way in which emerging black elites assert their belonging as equal citizens in the respective nations.

Finally, Annie Paul, Publications Officer, SALISES, UWI, examines the pervasiveness of skin bleaching amongst Indians in India. The article highlights the significant consumption of skin bleaching products by both men and women in India. The author argues that the consumption of skin lightening products in India is boosted by the large volume of advertisements that are aired or appear on various media, such as television, magazines and social media platforms.

As mentioned before, we feel that the politics of beauty and sexuality is not something that should be taken lightly. How beauty is defined, shaped and deployed in black communities, and how it is promoted and in many cases denigrated must be critically analysed if issues related to identity complexes, self-esteem problems and insecurities are to be overcome.

ACKNOWLEDGMENTS

The editors would like to express special thanks to the Office of the Principal and the Special New Initiative Grant Committee of the University of the West Indies, Mona for providing the necessary funds to produce this groundbreaking special issue of IDEAZ.

We would also like to thank the Florida International University Kimberly Green Latin American and Caribbean Center (FIU LACC) not only for providing support for this special issue by facilitating access to essential library materials and affording office space and the provision of stationery during the process of preparing this volume, but also for facilitating the contribution to this volume of a fascinating article from affiliated faculty member, Professor Jean Rahier, Director of the African and African Diaspora Studies Program at FIU.

In addition, we would like to extend special thanks to our editorial assistant and image consultant for this special issue of IDEAZ, Ms Kadine Ferguson. She played a major supportive role in the pre-production process of this special issue.

Not least, we offer heartfelt gratitude to the models, photographers and illustrators for their important contribution to this issue.

Figure G-2 • Hadeikaye Williams

HISTORICAL SOCIOLOGY OF BEAUTY PRACTICES

Internalized Racism, Skin Bleaching and Hair Straightening

IMANI M. TAFARI-AMA

Abstract   This article examines the practices of skin bleaching and hair straightening in order to explore the extent to which Africans (among other postcolonials) have internalized the dominant racist discourses informing popular notions of beauty and sexual desirability. The argument demonstrates that Afrikans who have experienced intergenerational, white supremacist conditioning, have come to reject all things Afrikan as denoted by the proverb which advocates that "anything too black nuh good". Skin bleaching and hair straightening are thus narratives indicative of self-hate. These performances of chemical self-transformation attest to the hegemonic complicity of victims of oppression with their own self-erasure.

Key words • Hair straightening • Skin bleaching • Self-hate
• White supremacist conditioning

IDEAZ Vol. 14 • 2016 • ISSN 0799-1401 (1–19)
© Centre for Tourism & Policy Research / Ian Boxill – UWI, Mona

UNHEALTHY BEHAVIOURS

The twin practices of skin bleaching and hair straightening are present-day indicators of the internalization and reproduction by Afrikan people – on the Continent and in the Diaspora – of racialized notions of embodied aesthetics, which are anchored in sexual and social meanings that are white defined and designed to reproduce white supremacist narratives of power and self-identity politics. According to Cheryl Thompson (2009), "Today, it is estimated that 70% to 80% of black women chemically straighten their hair. In the 1980s, weaves raised the black beauty bar even higher to hair that is not just straight, but also very long." Similarly, skin bleaching is rampant as an embodied performance of internalized racism (Tafari-Ama, 2006).

> More and more... Black women are bleaching their skin... in a bizarre attempt to acquire the psychosocial status associated with Brown or 'soially White' skin. This is a prominent example of how racist discourses of inscribed embodiment, which place particular emphasis on women's idealised sexual desirability, reflect the historical fracturing of Black identities (Tafari-Ama, 2006: 283).

We know that hegemony is at play (Gramsci, 1957) when those dominated by discourses of racial and ethnic disfigurement appropriate those myths and perform them as if they were their own. The prevailing political economy of notions of beauty and sexual desirability invalidates Afrikan embodiment and legitimizes a Eurocentric "look" and apparatus of dominance. This has resulted in an inversion of Afrikanness in order to promote a racialized global industry in so-called beauty products targeting women of Afrikan descent. Increasingly, men have also been incorporated into this discourse of cultural disfigurement and denigration.

Hegemony is also demonstrated by the fact that Afrikans and other people of colour, who have been dominated by discourses of racial and ethnic disfigurement since the onset of the Holocaust of Enslavement, mindlessly perform the myths of white supremacy, sold as "transformation" products and discourses, as if they were their own. It is obvious that there is huge institutional interest in people of Afrikan heritage being duped into thinking that they are subordinate to white and white identified people, as promoted in popular culture instruments such as the mass media of communication, including fashion magazines, television, newspapers, the World Wide Web, music and music videos, beauty contests and so on. It is therefore relevant to conjecture who is benefiting and who is hurt by this racialized politics of identity inversion.

When oppressed and exploited people such as the majority Afrikan class in Jamaica demonstrate inclinations to hegemony (Gramsci, 1957) with such self-hate practices as skin bleaching, hair straightening and weaving, it is clear that institutionalized racism is intact in the identity politics practised on the island, a microcosm of this world-wide dis-ease that denotes the traumatic legacy of colonialism (Leary, 2005). In this regard, Nehusi (2002) argues that "white supremacist stereotypes... imprison the minds and restrict the vision of so many who are often unaware that their vision has been engineered, their perceptions altered and their actions therefore predetermined by their enemies" (2002:5).

Hegemony is definitely at work when Afrikan people are using chemicals to lighten their complexions without caring about the harmful effects.

> Hydroquinone present in illegally imported skin bleaching products decreases melanin excretion from melanocytes and may also prevent its production. It is topically used as a de-pigmenting agent for the skin, which should be protected from sunlight to reduce re-pigmentation. In the United Kingdom, law permits use of this product up to 2% and limits the maximum concentration of hydroquinone in hair dyes and cosmetic products for localized skin lightening (Obuekwe and Ochei, 2004: 85).

Skin bleaching and chemical hair straightening practices are directly related to the hegemonic condition of internalized racism (Tafari-Ama, 2006). The Holocaust of European Enslavement of Afrikans, predicated on the use of racism as a mechanism of power and control (Mills, 1997), was undoubtedly the worst crime against humanity. This criminal apparatus was endorsed by heads of state, religious representatives, members of the wealthy class and was the basis for the construction of colonial empires from which their nationals benefited in one way or another. On the other hand, the deleterious effects that enslavement has had on psychosocial and physical health, on the socioeconomic status and development potential of Africa and her Diaspora are irrefutable and devastating. The United Nations declared 2015-2024 the International Decade for People of African Descent on the three-pronged platform of Recognition, Justice and Development, in acknowledgement of their colonial and postcolonial suffering. As Goodwill Ambassador Danny Glover said, citing UN Secretary-General Ban Ki-moon: "People of African descent are amongst those most affected by racism. Too often, they face denial of basic rights such as access to quality health services and education" (*UN News Center*, 2016).

The black body, and particularly its female embodiment, is the slate on which scripts of hegemonic narratives of identity politics have been inscribed as a result of the Maafa, the Holocaust of Enslavement (Nehusi, 2002) and its even more invidious postcolonial aftermath. Increasingly, however, men and children are practising this form of self-annihilation, with obviously deleterious implications for sustainable Afrikan posterity.

This article addresses the pervasive practices of skin bleaching, hair weaving and hair straightening, indicators of the psychosocial disorders resulting from enslavement (Hickling and Paisley, 2011; Nehusi, 2005), in order to understand the racist underpinnings of the mental enslavement denoted by such behaviours and, further, the internalization of racism (Agozino, 2015). Moreover, the postcolonial impact of internalized racism on the psychosocial health of the Afrikan majority class in postcolonial societies like Jamaica is directly related to the Holocaust of Enslavement and its colonial and postcolonial aftermath endured by Afrikans in the Americas and the Caribbean through systematic dehumanization for just over five centuries.

The article also aims to tackle social distinctions which have allowed self/other violence to become entrenched in self-representation behaviours in the majority Afrikan class in Jamaica. As noted elsewhere (Tafari-Ama, 2006: 285):

> The value system of embodiment that obtained in colonial and post-colonial Jamaica persists to this day, ensuring that the codes of colour-class definitions of privilege still inform the social locations of the races occupying this island polity. These hier-archies are even more magnified in the urban grassroots, with value-loaded distinctions being made among shades of Black, even to the extent of the self-destruction of melanin rich skin via bleaching agents. This practice represents both the result and the continuation of discriminatory definitions of racial embodiment; definitions that were constructed in plantation society.

THE UNDERLYING ROOTS (CAUSES) OF THESE UNHEALTHY BEHAVIOURS

Internalized racism (white supremacy) has had deleterious effects on Afrikan Jamaicans who constitute approximately 95 per cent of the Northern Caribbean island's population, with the result that the majority are in denial of their Afrikan heritage and, in fact, are anxiously preoccupied with representing themselves in performances that imitate a Eurocentric identity model, as manifested in the widespread twin practices of skin bleaching and hair straightening. This reveals the extent of the invidious Post Traumatic Slave Syndrome (Leary, 2005), the direct consequence of the Afrikan Holocaust and its neocolonial aftermath, which has distorted the psyche of Afrikan (Black) people (Eyerman, 2001; Hickling and Paisley, 2011; Leary, 2005; Reddock, 1990; Tafari-Ama, 2006), especially those living in poverty (Stone, 1973; Tafari-Ama, 2006). Europeans and Arabs and their continental

Afrikan accomplices who enslaved Afrikans (Nehusi, 2002) used racism as a belief system or doctrine to entrench notions of biological differences between the races as evidence of social and economic superiority of Europeans over Afrikans and other people of colour. This idea was brutally enforced – physically as well as psychologically, emotionally, spiritually and materially – with the disastrous outcome of over five centuries of exposure to institutionalized racism (Biney, 2013) and its attendant oppressions.

Maafa, the Holocaust of enslavement, undoubtedly the worst crime against humanity, caused a profound syndrome of mental enslavement (Leary, 2005; Nehusi, 2005), which has resulted in Afrikan people's reproduction and performance of racist stereotypes of beauty and, correspondingly, challenged the capacity of Afrikan people to reproduce positive self-concepts:

> The global white supremacist paradigm of beauty continues to promote European forms of beauty that African people consciously or unconsciously aspire to as a consequence of the pervasiveness of the white supremacist ideation system that controls everything from economics, political models of how power should be distributed in society, religion, and defines and controls how beauty is represented and who represents beauty (Biney, 2013).

Jamaica's excessively high murder rate (the third highest in the world) is tied to prevailing high levels of personality disorder (Hickling and Robertson-Hickling, 2013) and this, in turn, is directly related to the historical distortion of the nation's genesis and the fact that independence has not yielded a transformative model of governance (Tafari-Ama, 2006). The concept of personality disorder is therefore being used in this article to explore skin bleaching, hair weaving and straightening as expressions of mental enslavement (Nehusi, 2005) in order to analyse these dysfunctional embodied practices of so-called *beauty enhancement* as a form of social psychosis. This widespread practice of so-called enhancement actually constitutes chemical alteration of hair and skin texture in crude imitation of a European construct of beauty. The concept of personality disorder enables me to show that despite being emancipated and independent, Afrikans in the Diaspora whose ancestors experienced enslavement are so deeply trapped in the vortex of denial of Afrikan identity that it amounts to a psychosocial pathological condition. This conundrum is directly related to the colonial Holocaust:

> Afrikans have been largely mentally imprisoned by the continuing predominance of colonizing oppressors' notions of reality. Their very perceptions of themselves and their world is more often than not predetermined by a value system that is prejudiced against them and remains a hidden resident embedded in the very languages into which they have been indoctrinated (Nehusi, 2005: 12).

Appreciation of positive meanings associated with natural Afrikan hair has shifted to imitating Eurocentric hairstyles as a social norm, to the extent that an estimated 70–80 per cent of black women chemically straighten their hair (Thompson, 2009). On top of this, the practice of wearing weaves became distinctly pervasive among black women since the 1980s (Banks, 2000; Tate, 2009).

This psychotic behaviour will require the application of a profound project of social re-engineering to arrest, reverse and replace it with a sustainable development agenda, headlined by concerns for healing and cultural rehabilitation. This healing is dependent on the dispersal of the idea of self-reclamation contained in Marcus Garvey's injunction, "Up, up, you mighty race; you can accomplish what you will!" This appeal refutes the seemingly irreversible pattern of self-destruction into which the Afrikan race is currently inserted, after being exposed to the vicious, racist colonial machinery of the West (the notable exception being the Afrikan nation, Ethiopia).

The hegemonic turn of institutionalized racism is explicit in the international industry of so-called beauty products, which reify perceptions of social advantage in whiteness and reinforce the social distinctions created by colourism and shadism (Beckford and Witter, 1980; Biney, 2013). Those making these products are comprised of an empire of merchants intent on capitalizing on the systemic and psychosocial deformity of people of Afrikan heritage (Hickling and Paisley, 2011). The contemporary distorted Afrikan identity complex (Nehusi, 2005) denies Afrikan subjectivity, which is directly linked to the psychology of objectification projected onto Afrikans in the context of the Holocaust of enslavement or Maafa (Nehusi, 2005).

Organized religion, the anthesis of spirituality in general and Afrikan spirituality in particular, has been the principal mechanism that has been used – by colonial and postcolonial hegemonic regimes alike – to deploy a white supremacist discourse of self-identity, manifested in deliberately hierarchical arrangements of power, to trick people of Afrikan descent into schizophrenic embodied performances that guarantee their own annihilation. In this sense, organized religion can be seen as a discourse of violence (Tafari-Ama, 2006). During the Maafa, Afrikans were duped into regarding God as white, a mistaken notion that has passed largely uninterrogated through centuries of cultural reproduction. This anachronistic thought has translated in modernity into a ritualistic search for beauty through chemical designer products that rob Afrikan people of their melanin and electrified kinky hair.

The prevailing narrative of commodifiying beauty to transform Afrikan women into silky-tressed bleached-bodied pathetic imitations of Euro-Asian idealized beauty is not sustainable and poses a clear and present danger to the agency of Africans in the Diaspora and on the Continent. The hegemonic turn is that there is no human tragedy so profound as performing one's Afrikan body in self-destruction mode in an attempt to retrieve lost self-esteem in the idiom of a racialized, sexualized, classist and anti-Afrikan version of self-identity.

THE SOCIAL, ECONOMIC AND OTHER COSTS

In Jamaica, it is the norm for people of predominantly Afrikan descent to be seen with chemically straightened hair and bleached out faces, strutting their stuff with the attitude of having *arrived* or improved their social status. In many privileged as well as underserved communities, popular definitions of beauty and sexual desirability are conjugated in the racist hierarchy framework of a white or socially white minority at the peak of the prevailing socioeconomic pyramid and the majority class at the base (Beckford and Witter, 1980). Many citizens across this highly stratified spectrum have unquestioningly internalized the racist proverbial notion that "anything too black nuh good" (anything that is too black is not good).

On the other hand, hair straightening has long been a body altering practice among people of Afrikan heritage whose internalization of white supremacist myths about embodied aesthetics has resulted in intergenerational systems of self-denial, detrimental to Afrikan autonomy. The many "beauty" schools that operate in Jamaica – including the quasi-academic vocational training centre, the Human Employment and Resource Training

Agency (HEART Trust/NTA) – fail to interrogate the common practices of chemically altering skin colour and hair and the insertion of extensions as self-improvement methods that are taken for granted. This denotes the extent to which narratives of racism have been woven into the cultural fabric. It is bizarre to onlookers from outside these spaces that there is apparently no reservation that prevents those participating in this practice from wearing their bleaching cream face masks, apparently oblivious of the dissonance entailed in this performance.

It is also commonplace to see women tossing manes of woven tresses with the attitude that they can perform their bodies (Butler, 1990) in the idiom of their colonial and modern oppressors by way of exaggerated imitations. The ludicrous and shamefully blissful ignorance of the contradictions of these contrived enactments of embodied legitimacy may be interpreted as personality disorder (Hickling and Paisley, 2011; Hickling and Robertson-Hickling, 2013), mental enslavement (Nehusi, 2005) or hegemony (Gramsci, 1957). However conceptually located, self-hate consequences of enslavement have to be regarded as cultural trauma (Leary, 2005; Eyerman, 2001), which is a major impediment to sustainable development.

The global paradigm of beauty (Mills, 1997) continues to promote European forms of beauty that Afrikan people consciously or unconsciously aspire to as a consequence of the pervasiveness of the white supremacist ideation system that controls everything from economics to political models of how power should be distributed in society, to religion, and definitions of how beauty is represented and who represents beauty.

The embodied nexus of values, attitudes and behaviours determines how we view ourselves and our place in history and the relationship of that past to a sustainable future. The majority of Afrikans living in the Diaspora have no sense of self in relation to their Afrikan identity; by their embodied performances (Butler, 1990), they are hell-bent on configuring themselves in the image, speech, behaviours, political economy, socialization systems, institutions such as education and religion, which reproduce racist colonial values of identity.

The Holocaust of enslavement has bequeathed the progeny of disadvantaged and dispossessed Afrikans the questionable legacy of structured inequality in societies like Jamaica. Those who have emerged as the elite through the machinations of racialized politics and economics (Thomas, 1988) have consistently relegated this majority group to the base of a typically pyramidal socially stratified structure.

This tradition of disadvantage is relentlessly eating away the flesh and shedding the very lifeblood of the society, and reflects the corrupt historical and political practices that continue to govern the society (in spite of 53 years of independence). It is the principal threat to the production of positive identity perceptions. Embodied identities are, thus, sites of political and subjective contradictions and, as such, reflect the fact that "the body is central to the discourses of superiority/inferiority on which sexism and racism are based" (Allen, quoted in Barrow, 1998: 276).

Although power is not a discretely dichotomized black-and-white issue, as evidenced by inter and intra rivalries across the race spectrum, those responsible for establishing systems of social difference should be held accountable and made to compensate the disadvantaged for their cumulative identity confusion. This debate therefore places the issue of "accountability on... [in the context of] larger structures of domination (sexism, racism and class elitism) and [indicts] the individuals – often [socially] white, usually male, but not always – who are hierarchically placed to maintain and perpetuate values that uphold these exploitative and oppressive systems" (hooks, 1994a: 117).

The dehumanization of Afrikans by Europeans has come to express itself as pervasive loss of Afrikan identity, despite consistent resistance waged by those who refused to succumb to the racist profit-making agenda of the Holocaust of enslavement. This psychosocial abuse has been transferred intergenerationally and meanders through discourses (Foucault, 1980; Tafari-Ama, 2006) and applications of white supremacy (Mills, 1997).

In contemporary Jamaica, manipulating the racist narrative of physical differences through observation of shadism and colourism conventions (Biney, 2013) is fundamental to the maintenance of antagonistic power relations between the state elite classes (perceived as the political and socioeconomic centre of society) and the mass of the population (seen as peripheral). Thus, discourses of difference sustain ideological hegemonies of dominant over subordinate classes. In neocolonial spaces, such antagonistic social relations have distinct race/colour, class and gender implications (Mills, 1997).

On the Continent and in the Diaspora, Afrikan people, who are still suffering from the effects of slavery and colonialism, are so psychologically damaged that they need to be seen as *victims*. It is no wonder that they are still using chemicals to lighten their complexions and straighten their hair, without apparently caring about the harmful effects, or recognizing the psychosocial disfigurement that they are bringing onto themselves (Obuekwe and Ochei, 2004: 85).

Skin bleaching and chemical hair straightening practices are thus directly related to the syndrome of internalized racism (Nehusi, 2005; Agozino, 2015). The Holocaust of enslavement has had a deleterious impact on the collective and individual psyche, psychosocial and physical health, socioeconomic status and development potential of Africa and her Diaspora (Leary, 2005). What is even more alarming is the effectiveness of the dehumanization and self-concept disfigurement syndromes on which this Holocaust was predicated and which has dogged the progeny of the enslaved through time and space. This disfigurement has resulted in the evolution of multi-billion dollar industries in hair and skin products, laced with chemicals, that target women of colour who have already been duped through institutionalized narratives of identity misrepresentation to privilege European (i.e. white) "looks" as the benchmark of sexual and social desirability and, conversely, deny the efficacy of being Afrikan (i.e. Black). Chris Rock's documentary *Good Hair* (2009) provides enlightenment about the horrific conjugation of Afrikan aesthetic illegitimacy while promoting Eurocentric self-representation ideals as the norm for Afrikan people.

SOCIOECONOMIC FACTORS

States like Jamaica are complicit in the pathological practices of skin bleaching and hair straightening and weaving since, despite the official ban on these products, government officials still charge General Consumption Tax (GCT) on these imports. Class action suits against the state for failing to secure public safety are potentially pending, arising from such state endorsed legislative and public health failures. Doctors have maintained steady protest against the routine violation of pharmaceutical industry bans on the importation of the damaging products, to no avail. In fact, dermatologists are reporting that they have treated many cases in recent times. "We have treated many cases numbering in the thousands over the years and the numbers continue to increase because people feel they must look beautiful," says dermatologist, Dr. Neil Persadsingh.

Popular definitions of beauty, which denigrate Afrikan aesthetics while elevating Eurocentric values, demonstrate the hegemonic dilemma stymieing development of a sensibility of independence and embodied self-confidence. In Jamaica in 2013, over 1 billion Jamaican dollars (then at a rate of roughly J$100 to US$1) were spent on importing hair extensions, eyelashes, wigs and related paraphernalia of so-called beauty. This figure represents fourteen times more than what some of Jamaica's Caribbean neighbours spent importing similar products (*Jamaica Observer*, Business Section, November 1, 2013).

The practices of identity erosion indicated by this investment in false identity resources denote Afrikan self-denial, and provide vivid examples of the political economy of loss of Afrikan self-consciousness. Money that could be used to advance the sustainable development of individuals, families, communities, the nation is being wasted on chemically laced and identity erasing products, with the endorsement of wayward, self-interested leadership that is out of touch with ways of leveraging self-realization norms for the majority class, which would redound to the benefit of the nation as a whole. As discussed, the minority population owns the economy (Thomas, 1988) and is therefore not in need of the racial rehabilitation that the Afrikan heritage majority so urgently requires.

The prevailing cultural norm for postcolonial shipwrecked Africans living in spaces like Jamaica is thus constructed on the premise of multiple currents of internalized oppression. The existential turn is that there is no human tragedy so profound as a race of people being duped through various deliberate mechanisms into rejecting Afrikan identity and repudiating its efficacy by engaging in self-destructive "beauty" practices in an attempt to re-construct themselves as poor imitations of others, (re)producing a racialized, sexualized, classist and anti-Afrikan version of self-identity.

Exemplifying this contradiction, a study of young women at the University of Benin (Obuekwe and Ochei, 2004) reveals that black women have been known to bleach their skin using hydroquinone-based products – and even when dermatological side-effects were observed, they did not hinder the use of these agents.

The examples cited show the importance of employing a lateral analysis of the relationship between history and contemporary sociology – the past and the present are indissolubly intertwined in the reproduction of a pervasive Afrikan identity crisis. Furthermore, widespread underdevelopment in postcolonial states like Jamaica is demonstrative of state neglect of the inalienable rights of all citizens to a healthy environment, free from threats to citizen security, which also demands application of transitional justice responsibility. Hence the relevance, in the context of the United Nations' proclamation of 2015-2024 as the International Decade for People of African Descent, of Glover's statement (*UN News Centre*, 2016), echoing UN Secretary-General Ban Ki-moon (cf. p. 3, this article).

Addressing this same concern on the Afrikan continent where this residual reminder of colonial intervention is also part and parcel of the cultural landscape, as exemplified by widespread use of skin-bleaching chemicals, Obuekwe and Ochei (2004) argue that such undesirable products "can become carcinogenic on the skin after long-term use". They strongly recommend "follow-up action on educating these young girls on the health implications involved in the use of these pharmaceutical products".

Research findings reveal white supremacy interest in the manufacture and distribution of so-called beauty products, which are really designer Afrikan-self-erasure agents. It is significant to note in this regard that "Most of these cosmetics, which included creams, lotions and soaps, were imported from Europe" (Obuekwe and Ochei, 2004). Racialized notions of embodied aesthetics are thus anchored in Eurocentric connotations of embodiment and self-identity, which benefit a capitalist driven economy. This economy is white defined and is designed to reproduce white supremacist narratives of power and self-identity politics on black bodies (Tafari-Ama, 2006).

Weedon (1999) concurs, arguing that this pathology is entrenched in societies where institutionalized racism is the mainstay of the political economy.

PSYCHOSOCIAL ISSUES

The capitulation of the oppressed and exploited Afrikan majority class in Jamaica to the dominant discourse of internalized and institutionalized racism as denoted by the altering of their physical appearance to mimic perceptions of (social) whiteness also demonstrates the ideologial flimsiness of Jamaica's post-independence leadership, which has not instigated critical thinking about prevailing detrimental narratives of self-representation and misrepresentation.

As a result of being bombarded for centuries by institutionalized racism, classism, sexism and anti-Afrikanism, Afrikans living in spaces like Jamaica suffer from widespread shame about self-identity and the social, political, cultural and economic relevance of being Afrikan and embodying an Afrikan viewpoint. In order to enhance individual self-worth, self-confidence and self-esteem, the authorities need to create systems of social rehabilitation that empower the majority class to make choices that enhance personal and collective well-being.

Despite the sophistry of mannerisms of political participation in the world economy, Jamaica continues to engage on terms of inequality; the island's continued subservience to international capital and its inverted definitions of identity politics, demonstrated in sharp colour/class cleavages (Nettleford, 1978; Thomas, 1988), show all too clearly an absence of certitude about the legitimacy of Afrikan citizenship.

> In... societies where whiteness is hegemonic, skin colour and phenotype are inescapable markers of difference. However much an individual might want to escape racial categorization and be seen merely as an individual, s/he finds her/himself confined by white societies' implicit and explicit definitions of whiteness and racial otherness. These definitions are not merely the property of prejudiced individuals, they are structural, inhering in the discourses and institutional practices of the societies concerned (Weedon, 1999: 152).

There is the widespread perception in this context that in order to achieve the status that goes along with being brown (Stone, 1973; Tafari-Ama, 2006) or socially white (Beckford and Witter, 1980), one has to alter the way one wears their skin and the complexion that they project. As far as popular social beliefs are concerned, in order to achieve materiality and social acceptance, in order to fit in to the prevailing norm, people of predominantly Afrikan descent have to alter how they look. There is thus a direct connection between the absence or low level of an Afrikan centredness worldview and self-inflicted and social violence perceived as beauty enhancement practices via skin bleaching, hair weaving or straightening.

These behaviours reflect the unresolved cultural trauma of enslavement and prevailing identity loss among the Afrikan majority population in Jamaica. This embedded trauma (Leary, 2005), which appears to exist at the level of the unconscious, constitutes discursive denial of Afrikan connectivity.

Addressing this cultural crisis, Paul (2012) observes that:

> The bleaching or whitening of official Jamaican culture away from its African origins persists today and manifests itself in all sorts of ways from actual skin bleaching to the seamless assimilation of colonial norms, values and practices on the part of the middle and upper classes.

Evidence of this dysfunctional identity politics lies in the pervasive-ness of the embodiment alteration practices of skin bleaching, hair weaving and straightening as delusional expressions of "beauty". These practices are critically reviewed in this paper in order to deconstruct the neocolonial paradigm of so-called beauty enhancement as a form of social psychosis akin to personality disorder (Hickling, 2011).

RELIGION HIJACKS AFRIKAN IDENTITY

People of Afrikan descent were duped during enslavement into regarding God as white, a mistaken notion that has passed uninterrogated through centuries of cultural reproduction. This anachronistic thought has translated in modernity into a ritualistic search for beauty through chemical designer products that rob Afrikan people of their melanin and electrified kinky hair. This shows the extent to which persons of predominantly Afrikan ancestry have internalized and reproduced suicidal intersections of racism, sexism, classism and anti-Afrikanness. This syndrome of Afrikan self-denial provides the loom for weaving embodied tapestries of identity politics that provide the antithesis of self-realization.

The residue of unresolved cultural trauma of enslavement (Leary, 2005) appears to exist at the level of the unconscious. Discursive self-denial of Afrikan connectivity and the excuses about the unmanageability of one's Afrikan textured hair provides a recurring decimal for the rationalizations for practices of Afrikan self-erasure.

The theoretical assumption of this discussion is that the

linking of the past to the present (Eyerman, 2001) will facilitate critical examination of the causes and replay of unresolved traumatic events in the contemporary period (Leary, 2005; Nehusi, 2003), as denoted by these embodied indicators of identity genocide, which exemplify protracted mechanisms of institutionalized racist power. It interrogates the causes and manifestations of Afrikan identity loss and suggests that healing the breach as a model of psychosocial rehabilitation is critical for sustainable development to ensue at individual, family, community, national or global levels.

POSSIBLE SOLUTIONS

Prevailing problematic identity issues which pose threats to cultural development need to be urgently addressed in order to safeguard our posterity. Research aimed at benchmarking best practices for extrapolation to other environments with similar issues is also needed in order to alter the widespread dysfunctional identity representation practices. Ultimately, this exposé has the potential to raise consciousness about the problematic and catalyse a multisectoral approach to transformation at the policy making, implementation and subaltern power-broking and action levels. Institutions of socialization, including schools, faith-based institutions (FBIs), youth and sports clubs, mass media, the music industry, the political parties should all collaborate to redress the public health crisis posed by self-erasure practices like skin bleaching, hair straightening and weaving. Government officials should be encouraged to provide the material resources and entrepreneurial opportunities to ensure that public education efforts about this problematic are grounded in a sustainable framework.

Considering the foregoing, the problematic of individual, family, community, national and regional underdevelopment will not be resolved until a concerted effort is made to recover lost Afrikan identity. This recovery should be anchored in conscious-ness of who we are, above and beyond the dehumanized remnants of who we could have been, were it not for the Maafa.

This article also challenges established social distinctions, which have allowed self/other dichotomies to become entrenched in self-representation behaviours in the majority Afrikan class in Jamaica. The psychotic behaviours of skin bleaching and hair straightening and accessory practices of hair weaving and stylizations denote the entrenchment of internalized racism and the dominance of white supremacy, which will require the application of a profound project of social re-engineering to arrest, reverse and replace it with a sustainable development agenda, headlined by concerns for healing and cultural rehabilitation. It is high time for the healing to begin.

References

Agozino, Biko. 2011. Series Editor's Preface to *Apartheid Vertigo: The Rise in Discrimination Against Africans in South Africa*, by David M Matsinhe, xiii-xvi. England and USA: Ashgate. Retrieved April 28, 2015 (http://www.ashgate.com/pdf/SamplePages/Apartheid_Vertigo_Pref.pdf).

Akbar, Na'im. 1996. *Breaking the Chains of Psychological Slavery*. Tallahassee: Mind Productions & Associates.

Allen, C.F. 1998. Caribbean bodies: Representation and practice. In *Caribbean Portraits: Essays on Gender Ideologies and Identities*, ed. C. Barrow, 276-293. Kingston: Ian Randle Publishers; University of the West Indies, Mona: Centre for Gender and Development Studies.

Banks, Ingrid. 2000. *Hair Matters: Beauty, Power and Black Woman's Consciousness*. New York: New York University Press.

Barnett, M., ed. 2012. *Rastafari in the New Millennium*. New York: Syracuse University Press.

Beckford, G.L. 1972. *Persistent Poverty: Underdevelopment in Plantation Economies of the Third World*. New York, London, Toronto: Oxford University Press.

Beckford, G., and M. Witter. 1991. *Small Garden... Bitter Weed: Struggle and Change in Jamaica*. UWI, Mona: Institute of Social and Economic Research.

Biney, A. 2013. Ama Biney reviews documentary *Dark Girls*. Retrieved April 16, 2013 (http://www.pambazuka.net/en/category.php/books/89003).

Butler, J. 1990. *Gender Trouble: Feminism and the Subversion of Identity*. New York and London: Routledge.

Clarke, J. H. (14 June 2010: uploaded to YouTube) *Africa Before Slavery*. Africa profound series. Pt. 3. [S.l.]: Apco Productions.

Crenshaw, K. 1993. Mapping the margins: Intersectionality, identity politics, and violence against women of colour. *Stanford Law Review* 43:1241. Retrieved

May 1, 2015 (http://socialdifference.columbia.edu/files/socialdiff/projects/ ArticleMapping_the_Margins_by_Kimblere_Crenshaw.pdf).

DeGruy Leary, J. 2005. *Post Traumatic Slave Syndrome: America's Legacy of Enduing Injury and Healing.* Milwaukee, OR: Uptone Press.

Diop, Cheikh Anta. 1974. *The African Origin of Civilization: Myth or Reality.* Trans. M. Cook. New York: Lawrence Hill Books.

Eyerman, R. 2001. *Cultural Trauma: Slavery and the Formation of African American Identity.* Cambridge, NY: Cambridge University Press. Retrieved April 15, 2015 (https://books.google.com.jm/books?id = Vo1wmsvZA-oC).

Fanon, F. 1970. *Black Skin, White Masks.* London: Paladin.

Freire, P. 1972. *Pedagogy of the Oppressed.* London: Penguin.

Hickling, F.W. and H. Robertson-Hickling. 2013. Media representation of personality disorder in Jamaica: Public scholarship as a catalyst of health promotion. *West Indian Medical Journal* 62(5) (http://caribbean.scielo.org/scielo. php?pid = S0043 -31442013000500013&script = sci_arttext&tlng = en).

Gramsci, A. 1957, *The Modern Prince and Other Writings*, New York: International Publishers.

Hickling, F.W., and J. Paisley. 2011. Redefining personality disorder: A Jamaican perspective. *Rev Panam Salud Publica* 30(3).

Hickling, F. W., and G. Walcott. 2013. Personality disorder in convicted Jamaican murderers. *West Indian Medical Journal* 62(5):453-457.

hooks, b. 1994a. *Outlaw Culture: Resisting Representations.* New York and London: Routledge.

hooks, b. 1994b. *Teaching to Transgress: Education as the Practice of Freedom.* New York and London: Routledge.

Kim, R.M. 2007. Violence and trauma as constitutive elements in racial identity formation. Retrieved April 28, 2015. ProQuest (https://books.google.com. jm/books?id = b8bb5bsxvpMC).

Kozol, J. 1995. *Amazing Grace: The Lives of Children and the Conscience of a Nation.* New York: Crown Publishing Group.

Kwaku, Person-Lynn. 2014. On my journey now: The narrative and works of Dr. John Henrik Clarke, the knowledge revolutionary. *Journal of Pan African Studies* 6(7) (http://www.jpanafrican.org/docs/vol6no7/6.7-5Kwaku.pdf).

McIntosh, P. 1989. *White Privilege: Unpacking the Invisible Backpack.* Retrieved April 4, 2015 (https://www.isr.umich.edu/home/diversity/resources/white-privilege.pdf).

Mills, C. W. 1997. *The Racial Contract.* Ithaca and London: Cornell University Press.

Mohammed, Patricia. 1994, A social history of East Indian women in Trinidad from 1917 to 1947. Dissertation. U.W.I. St Augustine Campus.

Murrell, N. S., W. D. Spencer, and A. A. McFarlane, eds. 1998. *Chanting down Babylon: The Rastafari Reader.* Philadelphia: Temple University Press.

Nehusi, K. 2002. Mental enslavement. In *Emancipation,* ed. David Granger. Georgetown, Guyana (August).

Nehusi, K., ed. 2005. Soundscapes: Reflections on Caribbean oral and aural traditions. The University of the West Indies, Cave Hill Campus.

Nettleford, R. 1973. National Identity and Attitudes to Race in Jamaica. In *Consequences of Class and Colour: West Indian Perspectives*, ed. D. Lowenthal and L. Comitas, 35-56. New York: Anchor Books.

Nettleford, R. 1978. *Caribbean Cultural Identity: The Case of Jamaica*. Los Angeles: University of California.

Obuekwe, E. F., and U. M. Ochei. 2004. An epidemiological survey on the presence of toxic chemicals in soap and cosmetics used by adolescent female students from a Nigerian University. *Journal of International Women's Studies* 5(5):85-92.

Paul, A. 2012. Jamaica | bleached skin, white masks. *The Caravan*, 1 January. Retrieved April 5, 2015 (http://www.caravanmagazine.in/letters/ jamaica-bleached-skin-white-masks).

Racker, H. 1982. *Transference and Counter Transference*. London: Hogarth Press.

Reddock, R. 1986. Some factors affecting women in the Caribbean past and present. In *Women of the Caribbean*, ed. P. Ellis, 28-31. London and New Jersey: Zed Books Ltd.

Reddock, R. 1990. Towards an integrated analysis of race, class and gender in the Caribbean: Mixed materials. UWI, St Augustine Campus.

Reddock, Rhoda. 1996. Ethnic minorities in Caribbean society. Monograph. U.W.I., St Augustine Campus.

Rock, Chris, Kevin O'Donnell, Jeff Stilson, Lance Crouther, Chuck Sklar, Cliff-Charles, Marcus Miller, Roadside Attractions (Firm), HBO Films, ZahrloProductions, Urban Romances (Firm), Lions Gate Entertainment (Firm), et al. 2009. *Good Hair* [Motion Picture]. Santa Monica, Calif.: Lions Gate Entertainment.

Rowley, H., and E. Grosz. 1990. Psychoanalysis and feminism. In *Feminist Knowledge: Critique and Construct*, ed. S. Gunew, 175-204. London and New York: Routledge.

Stone, C. 1973. *Class, Race and Political Behaviour in Urban Jamaica*. UWI, Mona: Institute of Social and Economic Research.

Tafari, I. Jabulani. 1996. *A Rastafari View of Marcus Mosiah Garvey: Patriarch, Prophet, Philosopher*. Chicago: Greatcompany Inc.

Tafari-Ama, I. 1998. Rastawoman as rebel: Case studies in Jamaica. In *Chanting Down Babylon: The Rastafari Reader*, ed. N.S. Murrell, W.D. Spencer and A.A. Mc-Farlane, 89-106. Philadelphia: Temple University Press.

Tafari-Ama, I. 2006. *Blood Bullets and Bodies: Sexual Politics Below Jamaica's Poverty Line*. Kingston: Multi-Media Communications.

Tate, Shirley Ann. 2009. *Black Beauty: Aesthetics, Stylization, Politics*. Burlington, VT: Ashgate Publishing Company.

Thomas, C.Y. 1988. *The Poor and the Powerless: Economic Policy and Change in the Caribbean*. London: Latin America Bureau (Research and Action) Limited.

Thompson, C. 2008-2009. Black women and identity: What's hair got to do with It? Politics and performativity. *Michigan Feminist Studies* 22(1) (http://quod.

lib.umich.edu/cgi/t/text/text-idx?cc = mfsfront;c = mfs;c = mfsfront;idno = a rk5583.0022.105;rgn = main;view = text;xc = 1;g = mfsg).

UN News Center. 2016. Goodwill Ambassador Danny Glover calls out racism, Afrophobia in the Americas. Interview with Danny Glover. Feature. *UN News Center*, 30 June (http://www.un.org/apps/news/story.asp?NewsID = 54371 #.V-7wirUyfV2).

van Sertima, Ivan. [c. 1976] 2003. *They Came Before Columbus: The African Presence in Ancient America*. New York: Random House Trade Paperbacks.

Weedon, C. 1999. *Feminism Theory and the Politics of Difference*. Oxford and Massachusetts: Blackwell Publishers.

Wignall, M. 2011. Are you mentally disturbed too? *Jamaica Observer*, April 24. Retrieved May 3, 2015 (http://m.jamaicaobserver.com/mobile/columns/Are-you-mentally-disturbed-too-_8702339).

'I PREFER THE FAKE LOOK'

Aesthetically Silencing and Obscuring the Presence of the Black Body

CLINTON HUTTON

Abstract This article examines the definition, construction and cultivation of the ontology of white supremacy and the power it projected globally, based on one of its core arguments, the inherent aesthetic superiority of the European over the non-European, especially measured by the physicality and interiority of the European compared to the African. The article also examines how Africans in the Americas counteracted and or embraced white aesthetic construction of blackness in their struggles to be and suggests how this historical problematique of knowing and culturing aesthetic presence remains a central issue of sovereignty and decolonization in the 21st century.

Key words • White supremacy • Aesthetic • Sovereignty
• Decolonization

IDEAZ Vol. 14 • 2016 • ISSN 0799-1401 (20–32)
© Centre for Tourism & Policy Research / Ian Boxill – UWI, Mona

One of the major tenets of the system of ideas imagined, manufactured and woven into the superstructural landscape of the dystopian world of black inferiority, the foundational stone of white supremacy which defined the modern world, has to do with the alleged nature of the aesthetic complex of the human being and its relationship to knowing, identity, agency, power and authority. Hence the servile subjection of the African to the European was, to a large extent, justified in narratives of the alleged aesthetic superiority of the European over the African.

Here a simple logic in mainstream European racist aesthetic complex is proffered:

Beautiful people have the natural right to rule over ugly people. White people are beautiful while black people are ugly. Therefore, white people have the inherent right to rule over black people.

The aesthetic complex of the African vis-à-vis that of the European as an argument for white domination and the means to achieve, institute and maintain it, is replete with the epistemic culture of white supremacy as an immutable truth.

On this matter, Thomas Jefferson, author of the preamble to the constitution of the United States of America, which states that "All men are created equal…", says in his 1787 book, *Notes on the State of Virginia,* that the aesthetic difference between the African and the European, which made the African inferior and the European superior, was "fixed in nature". That is to say, the aesthetic state of the African compared to the European, with all the social and political consequences flowing from such, was objectively determined and thus independent of the will. Commencing with the difference in colour between black and white, Jefferson constructs a narrative of inequality based on values he attaches to supposedly superior aesthetic signs on the white body and their absence in the black body.

> Whether the black of the negro resides in the reticular membrane between the skin and the scarf-skin, or in the scarf-skin itself; whether it proceeds from the colour of the blood, the colour of the bile, or from that of some other secretion, the difference is fixed in nature… And is this difference of no importance? Is it not the foundation of a greater or less share of beauty in the two races? Are not the fine mixtures of red and white, the expressions of every passion by the greater or less suffusions of colour in the one, preferable to that external monotony, which reigns in the countenances, that immoveable veil of black which covers all the emotions of the other race? Add to these, flowing hair, a more elegant symmetry of form, their preference of them, as uniformly as is the preference of the Oran-ootan for the black women over those of his own species. The circumstance of superior beauty, is thought worth attention in the propagation of our horses, dogs, and other domestic animals; why not in that of man? (Eze, 1997: 97-98).

Meanwhile, Frenchman Georges Léopold Cuvier published an essay in his *Animal Kingdom* (1797) in which he affirmed: "The Caucasian, to which we belong, is distinguished by the beauty of the oval formed by its head, varying in complexion and the colour of the hair" (Eze, 1997: 104). "To this variety," Cuvier notes, "the most highly civilized nations, and those which have generally held all others in subjection, are indebted for their origin" (p. 104). As for the African, Cuvier states:

> The Negro race… is marked by a black complexion, crisped or woolly hair, compressed cranium, and a flat nose. The projection of the lower parts of the face, and the thick lips, evidently approximate it to the monkey tribe; the hordes of which it

Figure 2-1 • Arielle Henry

consists have always remained in the most complete state of barbarism (Eze, 1997: 105).

Here power, authority and civilization are the agential consequences of beautiful people. In the two examples given above, both Jefferson and Cuvier linked the aesthetic features of the exterior corporeal body to a corresponding state of intrinsic values associated with moral and ethical agency, civility, rationality, creativity, the sublime and the making of civilization on the one hand, and the very opposite of these values on the other hand. For Cuvier, "a black complexion, crisped woolly hair, compressed cranium, and a flat nose" represented "the most complete state of barbarism", while "the beauty of the oval formed by its head, varying in complexion and the colour of the hair" made the European the agency of "the most highly civilized nations". And for Jefferson, as a result of the "less share of beauty" in the African, he was yet to "find that a black had uttered a thought above the level of plain narration [or] even an elementary trait of painting or sculpture" (Eze, 1997: 99).

The notion of an inherent deformed or pathological aesthetic agency and creative ethos in the African is well documented and articulated in modern Western thought. Here the African in consequence of his exterior and interior ugliness, was incapable of appreciating or creating aesthetically pleasing art. He was unable to create works of art beyond the trifle, beyond the whimsical or art befitting of the beautiful (European). On account of his natural aesthetic deformity, he was not only unable to appreciate real art but the finer things in life generally. This made it easier for the European to deny the existence of real art from an African creative ethos since antiquity. Moreover, some African art was passed off as the work of people who were not African because Africans were not deemed capable of creating such art. At the same time, a lot of African/African diaspora artistic expressions were banned or otherwise proscribed as crude, vulgar, whimsical, infantile, and of the devil. At the same time, African art was pillaged and stocked and displayed in European museums and galleries and private collections.

European racist epistemic and ontological construction of Africans and their creative ethos to justify their subjection provided the basis for statements such as the one made in 1854 by Andrew Foote, Commander of the United States Navy.

> If all the negroes of all generations were to be obliterated from recollection forever, the world would lose no great truth, no profitable art, no exemplary form of life. The loss of all that is African would offer no memorable deduction from anything but the earth's black catalogue of crimes (Pim, 1866: 9).

This type of attitude pretty much centred the emphatic culture of white supremacy so that whiteness could exist and enjoy the fruits and legacy of vile oppression without facing a moral crisis.

In the definition of the 'Negro' in the first American edition of *Encyclopaedia Britannica* (1798), the approach which Jefferson and Cuvier employed – linking the aesthetic state of the exterior body to a set of intrinsic values associated with the ontology and agency of barbarism and savagery on the one hand and civilization, rationality and high art on the other hand – is quite evident:

> Negro, *Homo pelli nigra,* a name given to a variety of the human species, who are entirely black, and are found in the torrid zone, especially in that part of Africa which lies within the tropic. In the complexion of negroes we meet with various shades; but they likewise differ far from other men in all the features of their face. Round cheeks, high cheek-bones, a forehead somewhat elevated, a short, broad, flat nose, thick lips, small ears, ugliness, and irregularity of shape, characterize their external appearance. The negro women have their loins greatly depressed, and very large buttocks, which give the back the shape of the saddle (Eze, 1997: 93-94).

Within this external appearance of the black body described above, is a corresponding set of moral, psychological, aesthetic, creative and cognitive values denoting the ontological and agential complex of the African:

> Vices the most notorious seem to be the portion of this unhappy race: idleness, treachery, revenge, cruelty, impudence, stealing, lying, profanity, debauchery, nastiness, and intemperance, are said to have extinguished the principles of natural law, and to have silenced the reproofs of conscience. They are strangers to every sentiment of compassion, and are an awful example of the corruption of man when left to himself (Eze, 1997: 94).

Here as in countless other instances, the case is made to justify the enslavement and colonial subjection of the supposedly aesthetically inferior African to the supposedly aesthetically superior European, because if left unsupervised by the beautiful, the pathological values and agency of the ugly will greatly multiply the pathological state of their zoological existence. The definition of the so-called Negro which is filtered through a racist Eurocentric aesthetic linguistic lens, not only locates the African in a state of nature of a perpetual dystopian Hobbsian type, which Georg Hegel called a "zoological garden", where he "lived in an animal condition of innocence" (Eze, 1997: 128). The African existed aesthetically and hence, cognitively, mentally, morally, psychologically and sexually in a state of nature. He was an unevolved, unhistorical being whose human nature did not make it possible for him to exit the state of nature on his own agency. This task became the white man's burden.

An ontologically unfree body which was the embodiment of the state of nature did not/could not belong to a free society/a state of man, since the agency of free society was contingent on the existence of an ontologically free body. The aesthetic embodiment of a free body and hence of a free society was the European – especially the European male whose burden it was to transport the ontologically unfree body into free society (where it remained unfree) under a perpetual regime of control and supervision to ensure its usefulness to civilization by preventing it from falling back into the state of nature.

This regime of control and supervision was a ceaseless state of coercion, of violence, intimidation and regimentation, of laws and social, cultural and ideological conditioning to manifest the linguistic cues, vision and meanings of the place and role of imagined white-blackness in the world created by whiteness. In this world the French slave maker Hilliard d'Auberteuil tells us that: "Policy and safety require that we crush the race of Blacks by a contempt so great that whoever descends from it to the sixth generation shall be covered with an indelible stain" (Rogers, 1994: 99).

What happened in this world that whiteness created to make d'Auberteuil's policy statement become flesh – that Africans would be so stained with a contempt for themselves that was so great that they would, on their own accord, pass it on from generation to generation, so that almost six generations after slavery was abolished in Jamaica, I grew up in a culture where I was made to understand that black was inferior? I also became aware of some of the expressions of this state of inferiority and the rituals performed to ameliorate the stained aesthetic cues of blackness (i.e. adopting aesthetic symbols of whiteness) in my community, which was almost to a person, entirely black. This of course was not the only tradition in my community for there were people who did not buy into the European aesthetic construction of blackness, which others have seen fit to internalize and pass on over these generations. There was thus the development of a black anti-slavery/anti-colonial tradition that sternly resisted the policy articulated by d'Auberteuil and advanced their own epistemology, aesthetic compass and philosophy of being.

In the world created by whiteness, the contempt for blackness was pervasively visible. Africans were forced to eat human excrement. In 1756 in Egypt, Westmoreland, Jamaica, slaveholder Thomas Thistlewood, wrote in his diary what he ordered done to "Port Royal", an enslaved man, for escaping:

> Gave him a moderate whipping, pickled him well, and made Hector shit in his mouth, immediately put in a gag whilst his mouth was full & made him wear it 4 to 5 hours (Hall, 1989: 72).

In another example, Governor Pinfold the British governor of Barbados, ordered in 1764, the sacrificial killing of "the slave Sharper" who was found "guilty" of raping and murdering Sarah Sutton, a white woman. Pinfold directed that Sharper be

> chained to a stake to be fixed for that purpose. That his privy members be cut off and burned before his face and that afterwards he be burned alive... the whole carcase be reduced to ashes and those ashes dispersed in the air that no part of such a villain may remain, and that the execution may be performed with such solemnity that it may strike the spectator with the greatest awe and terror (Watson, 1985: 6).

In the meanwhile, one eyewitness on a slave ship tells us that the captain for that ship, in order to "strike fear in the rest, killed a slave and dividing heart, liver and entrails into 300 pieces made each of the slaves eat one, threatening those who refused with the same torture. Such incidents were not rare" (James, 1989: 9).

And from Mississippi in the United States of America, "Marse Easterlin, the slaveholder, punished one of the men he owned by attaching him "day by day" like a horse to a plough and made him plough the field until he expired. According to Vinnie Busby whom Easterlin also owned, the slaveholder

> Took dat darkie an' hitched him to a plow an' plowed him jes' lak a hors. He beat him an' jerked him 'bout 'till he got all bloody an' sore, but ole Marse he kept right on day after day. Finally de buzzards went flyin' over 'em… dem buzzards kept a flyin' and ole Marse kept on a plowin' him 'till one day he died (Berlin, Favreau and Miller, 1998: 15-16).

In Dutch Guiana (Suriname), one 14-year-old enslaved boy, Cadety, was punished for an entire year by his owner, one "Mr. Ebbers":

> For the space of a whole year, by alternately flogging him for one month, then keeping him laid flat on his back with his feet in the stocks for another, then making him wear an iron triangle called a pot-hook around his neck, to prevent him for escaping or sleeping for a third month, and chaining him to the landing place in a dog's collar night and day without shelter, with orders to bark at every boat or canoe that passed for a fourth, etc., etc., till the youth had almost become insensible to his sufferings, walked crooked and, in a manner, degenerated into a brute (Price and Price, 1992: 147).

These acts/rituals of exemplary punishment and many other other categories of such, were designed to frame the existential psychological, emotional and ontological path not only of the immediate victims but even more so the community of Africans in general and to signal to Europeans the ontological difference and the boundary of their emphatic culture for black people. Georg Hegel articulates this well:

> The Negro is an example of animal man in all his savagery and lawlessness, and if we wish to understand him at all, we must put aside all our European attitudes. We must not think of a spiritual God or moral laws; to comprehend him correctly… nothing consonant with humanity is to be found in his character. For this very reason, we cannot properly feel ourselves into his nature,

no more than into that of a dog…. Only by means of thought can we achieve this understanding of his nature; for we can only feel that which is akin to our own feelings (Eze, 1997: 127-128).

These acts were designed to devalue the humanity and self-confidence of blackness in itself and to render in its existential ethos an ontology of obedience and subordination in thought, mind and body (praxis) to the sovereignty of whiteness. If enslaved Africans could be made to feel that their person was of little or no value to themselves but only a tool in the service of whiteness, then what would be the use of fighting for freedom and justice? What would be the use of fighting to protect, preserve and empower such diminishing ontological presence, whose contribution to the world was the "earth's black catalogue of crimes"?

Every one of those categories of ritual performances to aid the ontological desecration of the black body to convert it into a tool in the service whiteness, had its cognitive, ideological and linguistic counterpart. A classic example of this articulation of the combined use of force with that force of epistemic and linguistic expression, was articulated by renowned African American abolitionist Frederick Douglass thus:

> To make a contented slave, you must make a thoughtless one. It is necessary to darken his moral and mental vision, and, as far as possible, to annihilate his power of reason. He must be able to detect no inconsistencies in slavery. The man that takes his earnings, must be able to convince him that he has a perfect right do so. It must not depend on mere force; the slave must know no Higher Law than his master's will. The whole relationship must not only demonstrate, to his mind, its necessity, but its absolute rightfulness (Douglass, 1969: 320).

And so the epistemic, linguistic and metaphorical expressions of force, i.e., the arguments created by whiteness to convince the African of his inherent servile state, of which his aesthetic state was a main example, were as important as the physical/psycho-physical force imposed on the black body. Indeed both of them were often used simultaneously. And they both jointly engendered the ontology of stain in black existence, so much so that it was recognized in the black experience by some people of African descent as a stumbling block in the struggle to become. Haitian revolutionary and statesman Valentin Vastey, for example, addressed the deep existential social and political psychology of this issue in the early 19th century when some black and brown people joined forces with Napoleon Bonaparte's counterrevolutionary troops to destroy the Haitian Revolution in 1803 in order to restore slavery. Vastey referred to those black and brown Haitians as "these indigènes, Blacks and Mulattoes in their outward complexion alone, but ex-colonialists in hearts and principle [who] were and yet are, the most inveterate enemies of their brethren and their country [who] deserve to be slaves" (Vastey, 1969: 30).

In May 1865, James Lynch also addressed this issue at a meeting of the Young Men's Literary and Debating Society of Philadelphia in the United States of America. According to Lynch, in an address appropriately titled "Colored Men Standing in the Way of Their Race":

> It is strange, but true, that we have such men among us... who set no value on the ability of their race and adopt the opinions respecting them that prejudiced white men hold.... They are studious in disparaging their own color, and paying homage to a supposed native superiority of the whites (Foner, 1972: 317).

Here Lynch finds it "strange" that some black men would marginalize themselves and their own people by accepting as true the racist European notion of black inferiority and white superiority. Moreover, Lynch tells us of another class of black men

> who pride themselves on the color of their skins, feeling that a light complexion imparts superiority. It is questionable whether there is in existence a more contemptible feeling than this, for while it assumes superiority over the darker skin, it confesses inferiority to the lighter, or white, person (Foner, 1972: 317).

These views, in Lynch's logic, reflect a social being using the arguments of white prejudice to construct a relationship of superiority over persons of his own race he deemed racially inferior and thereby fetter the cohesion/solidarity necessary to combat slavery/colonialism and its culture of prejudice.

At the beginning of the 20th century, the Jamaican brown medical doctor and author, Theophilus Scholes, writes about the "Europeanized Ethiopian" and the problematique associated with him and the fight of people of African descent for freedom, equality, sovereignty and dignity. States Scholes:

> Having, from the dawn of consciousness upwards, been taught to associate with the white skin everything possessing superior merit, he ends up with the conviction that he himself is but a mass of demerit and inferiority; and so, upbraiding his Maker for the 'curse of a black skin', instead of the 'blessing of a white skin', for the 'curse of curly hair', instead of the 'blessing of straight hair', for the 'curse of black eyes', instead of the 'bless-

ing of blue eyes', he journeys through life, ashamed of himself and of every other member of his race. But this is an abnormal type of being, every person who is normal, whether he be called a savage or whether he be a product of the schools, instinctively loves his race (Scholes, 1905: 60).

In the three examples cited above, persons of African descent who have articulated and displayed behaviours apparently rooted in an internalization of European racist epistemology and ontology, were deemed to be in an abnormal psychological state, in the black philosophy of being (ontology or metaphysics) that emerged from black people's fight to be, since slavery. These persons with "contemptible feeling" for themselves and people like themselves, who were "ex-colonialists in their hearts and principle", betrayed an "abnormal type of being", which persons in the movement led by Paul Bogle in Jamaica in 1865, called "black skin white heart". These Europeanized Ethiopians, in my reading of Lynch and Scholes and others, have been imagining, ritualizing and cultivating a state of ontological redemption by disparaging themselves and associating their state of being with the white racist ontological body and its stated values as a way of obviating, dismembering/ not remembering their cursed, ugly, shameful body and to assume some measure of respectability, visibility and superiority over the obscured African body.

It is in this context that we can view the following statement made by the young African Jamaican woman, Justina, of the kind of child she would like to have when she became a mother. This statement was carried in Alice Spinner's 1894 novel, *A Study in Colour,* in which Justina was a character:

> I nebber could lub a black little chile same as I do the white. I worship de little massa an' if I lucky, ebe I may hab a fair chile one day. Not ob course a real white one, dat asking too much, but still one dat is almost white, an' den I worship it, an' work for it fe true. Dress it nicely too, in clean white clothes, wid shoes an' all, jest like a Buckra baby… I hope I nebber hab a black or dark chile to shame me (p. 52).

This statement fits well the Jamaican aphorism: "Ev'ry Jang Kro tink im pikni wyiit" (Every John Crow thinks his child is white). For Justina, it was aspiring for a child that "is almost white", one that would not have brought shame on her due to that child's black or dark complexion but one that would bring status, visibility and pride in her life because of its almost white presence. More broadly speaking, every John Crow (black bird that feeds on carrion), every black parent wants the best for her child – and that is best exemplified or measured by the status/achievements/certitude of white people.

There is a pragmatic logic to the aesthetic and broad ontological discarding of the black body by some people of African descent. It is the rejecting, discarding or escaping of a body that was marked for enslavement, brutality, disdain, disparagement, hate, prejudice, injustice, invisibility, obscurity, ridicule, subservience and lack of opportunity. In this sense the rituals of acquiring symbols and signs of success and respectability associated with the perceived white ontological order can be seen as a struggle for freedom by the discarding or masking of the black body. Additionally, this masking/discarding of what is deemed to be ontological Africa in the black body helps to allay presumed white fear and acquired black fear of the black body and possibly assist in the opening up of the avenues of opportunity perceived to be closed to the un-choreographed African body.

Masking is a far more sophisticated technological and scientific beauty business today compared to the balmy days of slavery, when women of African descent working in the great house first started using the solution they used to clean the slaveholders' floor to bleach their faces. Justina was intent to acquire status and satisfaction by getting pregnant for a man that would ensure that she gave birth to a child that "is almost white", remains unchanged. But like the modern skin-do (bleaching/toning) techniques, the hairdo techniques have also seen some developments which have some of their roots in the type of rhetoric and praxis Spenser St. John described and editorialized in Haiti in 1863:

> The principal trouble to the female negro mind is her unfortu-nate wool. How she envies her more favoured sisters their long tresses! How she tries to draw out each fibre, and endeavours to make something of it by carefully platting it with false hair! Even the smallest negro servant will spend hours in oiling, brush-ing, and tending this poor crop, whose greatest length will only compass three or four inches. It is only when women are more than half white that the wool turns into hair, and even then it has sometimes a suspicious crispy wave, which, however, looks well. Of later years chignons have been a regular importation from France, and the little negresses are delighted with them (St. John, [1884]1971: 150).

That the ideational and practical ontological desecration of the black body continues in rhetoric, hairdo, skin do and other dos and is often articulated as expressions of freedom and universalism into the first decade and a half of the 21st century, says much about the enormity and the depth of the stain in the epistemic and ontological culture of people of African descent even beyond the sixth generation. But it also shows the depth to which this continues in the generational culture of white expectation. And the meanings and messages used to advertise certain "hair care/skin care" products aimed at obscuring/masking/altering Africa in the black body in the 21st century are rooted, as ever, in the same racist aesthetic complex of slavery and colonialism. Only now the messages are clothed and delivered in a more polite speak.

References

Berlin, Ira, Marc Favreau, and Steven F. Miller, eds. 1998. *Remembering Slavery: African Americans Talk about their Personal Experiences of Slavery and Emancipation*. New York: The New Press in association with the Library of Congress, Washington D.C.

Douglass, Frederick. [1855] 1969. *My Bondage and My Freedom*. New York: Dover Publications.

Eze, Emmanuel Chukwudi, ed. 1997. *Race and the Enlightenment: A Reader*. Cambridge, Massachusetts and Oxford: Blackwell Publishers.

Foner, Philip S., ed. 1972. *The Voice of Black America: Major Speeches by Negroes in the United States, 1797-1971*. New York: Simon and Schuster.

Hall, Douglas. 1989. *In Miserable Slavery: Thomas Thistlewood in Jamaica, 1750-86*. London & Basingstoke: MacMillan Publishers.

James, C.L.R. [1963] 1989. *The Black Jacobins: Toussaint L'Ouverture and the San Domingo Revolution*. New York: Vintage Book.

Pim, Bedford. 1866. *The Negro and Jamaica*. London: Trübner and Co.

Price, Richard, and Sally Price, eds. 1992. *Stedman's Surinam: Life in an Eighteenth-Century Slave Society: An Abridged, Modernized Edition of Narrative of a Five-Year Expedition Against the Revolted Negroes of Surinam by John Gabriel Stedman*. Baltimore and London: The Johns Hopkins University Press.

Rogers, J.A. [1942] 1994. *Sex and Race: A History of White, Negro, and Indian Miscegenation in the Two Americas*. Vol. II. St. Petersburg; Florida: Helga M. Rogers.

Scholes, Theophilus E. 1905. *Glimpes of the Ages or the "Superior" and "In-ferior" Races, So-Called, Discussed in the Light of Science and History*. Vol. 1. London: John Long.

Spinner, Alice. 1894. *A Study in Colour.* London: T.F. Unwin.

St. John, Spenser. [1884] 1971. *Hayti; or the Black Republic.* London. Frank Cass & Co. Ltd.

Vastey, Baron de Pompée-Valentin. [1823] 1969. *An Essay on the Causes of the Revolution and Civil Wars of Hayti, being A Sequel to the Political Remarks upon French Publications and Journals concerning Hayti.* Tr. from French by W.H. M.B. New York: Negro Universities Press.

Watson, Karl. 1985. *Slave Executions on Barbados in the Eighteenth Century – An Analysis.* University of the West Indies, Mona, Jamaica: Department of History.

LATIN AMERICAN HYPER-SEXUALIZATION OF THE BLACK BODY

Personal Narratives of Black Female Sexuality/Beauty in Quito, Ecuador*

JEAN MUTEBA RAHIER

Abstract In this article, I focus on the way sexuality – a fundamental aspect of identities – has been negotiated and re-negotiated by Afro-Ecuadorian women within what I call the Ecuadorian "racial-spatial order" from the perspective of the particular local context of Quito, the capital city of Ecuador, at the end of the 1990s and at the beginning of the 2000s. My approach is two-fold: First, I examine the reproduction of stereotypical representations of black females as hyper-sexualized beings in Ecuadorian society, or in what could be called the "Ecuadorian commonsense". Second, I analyse the narratives of sexual life history that four Afro-Ecuadorian women residing in Quito shared with me between 1997 and 2001, during long conversations.

Key words • Sexuality • Hyper-sexualized • Stereotypical representations • Black females

IDEAZ Vol. 14 • 2016 • ISSN 0799-1401 (33–68)
© Centre for Tourism & Policy Research / Ian Boxill – UWI, Mona

This study focuses on the way sexuality – a fundamental aspect of identities – has been negotiated and re-negotiated by Afro-Ecuadorian women within what I call the Ecuadorian "racial-spatial order" from the perspective of the particular local context of Quito, the capital city of Ecuador, at the end of the 1990s and the beginning of the 2000s. The premise here is that identities are multiple, multifaceted, and non-essential; they are performed and performed anew within evolving socioeconomic and political situations, following personal or individual preferences and decisions. This requires us to view blackness in terms of personal, social, cultural, political, and economic processes embedded in particular time-space contexts, which are constituted within local, regional, national, and transnational dimensions.

My approach is two-fold: First, I examine the reproduction

of stereotypical representations of black females as hyper-sexualized beings in Ecuadorian society, or in what could be called the Ecuadorian "commonsense". Second, I analyse the narratives of sexual life history that four Afro-Ecuadorian women residing in Quito shared with me between 1997 and 2001, during long conversations. This examination provides not only the opportunity to appreciate the effects that these racist, stereotypical representations have had on the lives of these women, it also allows us to uncover the way these four women – as sociopolitical and sexual agents – have developed different strategies for pleasures and positive self-construction within a particular racist society. The focus is on the interface between the personal and the structural or societal, between self-presentation and interpellation. Indeed, the research reveals that different individuals or agents submitted to the same socioeconomic and political reality make different choices, which always express an original combination of both resistance and accommodation or adaptation to this reality (Foucault, 1975, 1978; Butler, 1997).

Before looking in detail at how black female bodies are objectified, sexualized and stereotyped in Ecuador, it might be useful to first look at current Ecuadorian racial and ethnic dynamics and their history.

THE PASSAGE FROM MONOCULTURAL *MESTIZAJE* TO MULTICULTURALISM

In Ecuador, as in other Latin American national contexts, white and white-mestizo urban and national elites have imagined or invented the national identity around the notion of *mestizaje* (race mixing). These elites have reproduced an "Ecuadorian ideology" of national identity that proclaims the mestizo (mixed race individual who has both European [Spanish] and Indigenous ancestry) as the prototype of modern Ecuadorian citizenship. This ideology is based on a belief in the indigenous population's inferiority, and on an unconditional – although sometimes contradictory – admiration and identification with occidental civilization (Stutzman, 1981; Whitten, 1981; Silva, 1995).

Despite this hegemonic attempt at racial and ethnic homogenization, the Ecuadorian ideology of national identity results in a racist map of national territory: urban centers (mostly Quito, Guayaquil, and Cuenca) are associated with modernity, while rural areas are viewed as places of racial inferiority, violence, backwardness, savagery, and cultural deprivation. These areas, mostly inhabited by non-whites or non-white-mestizos, have been viewed by the elites as representing major challenges to the full national development toward the ideals of modernity. For Ecuador, *Mestizaje*, as Whitten (1981) explains, does not mean that the white indianizes himself or herself but that, on the contrary, the Indian whitens himself or herself "racially" and culturally: the official imagination of Ecuadorian national identity "[is] an ideology of *blanqueamiento* within the globalizing framework of mestizaje" (Whitten, personal communication).

In this official imagination of Ecuadorian-ness, there is logically no place for blacks: they must remain peripheral. Afro-Ecuadorians – who represent about ten percent of the national population – constitute the ultimate Other, some sort of a historical accident, a noise in the ideological system of nationality, a pollution in the Ecuadorian genetic pool. The best example of "non-citizenship", they are not part of official *mestizaje*, unlike Indigenous peoples (Muratorio, 1994). In the logic of the national racial/spatial order, the two "traditional" regions of blackness (both developed during the colonial period) – the Province of Esmeraldas and the Chota-Mira Valley – are looked down upon by whites and white-mestizos. This is what Peter Wade (1993) calls "cultural topography".

Since the early 1990s, following the adoption of multicultural policies specifically targeting Indigenous and African diasporic populations by institutions of international development and global governance (the United Nations, the World Health Organization, etc.) (Hale, 2004, 2006), and also as a result of the political activism of Indigenous and African diasporic communities (de la Torre, 2006a), many Latin American nation-states revised their constitutions and sometimes passed special laws that expressed a concern for greater inclusion of African diasporic and Indigenous populations. It is in that context that the "allowed Indian" or the "permitted Indian identity" (*el indio permitido*) emerged (Hale, 2004), and Latin American African diasporic populations gained relatively greater agency in comparison to the marked exclusion or construction as (ultimate) Others (Rahier, 2013, 2014) that characterized their situation during what could be called "monocultural mestizaje" (Ibarra Dávila, 2002; Silva, 1995; Polo, 2002; Espinosa Apolo, 2003) – which roughly extended, for Ecuador, from the early 20th century through to the major *levantamientos indígenas* (Indigenous uprisings) of the early 1990s (Whitten et al., 2003; Clark and

Becker, 2007), culminating in the enactment in 1998 by the National Constitutional Assembly of a constitution that celebrated multiculturalism. A new Constitution, seen as going even further in the direction of multiculturalism, was adopted in 2008 by the newly established Constituent Assembly (Rahier, 2014).

The place of blackness within/outside Ecuadorian national identity continues to be ambiguous despite the multicultural turn formally officialized with the adoption of the 1998 Constitution (Rahier, 2014). With the analyses of visual representations of black women, I refer to the long history of black exclusion from the dominant Ecuadorian understanding of the nation during monocultural mestizaje and its metamorphosis into multiculturalism, which provides a genealogy for today's spontaneous representations of Ecuadorian and other black women that can be found on the Internet and in the daily press. I reach the conclusion that even though some notable changes have occurred since the "multicultural turn", there are also profound ideological continuities. Elsewhere, I have argued that in fact with multiculturalism, mestizaje – as an ideological technology of the state and as a project of the Ecuadorian elites – has not disappeared from the political landscape but instead continues to do its work both within and around multiculturalism (Rahier, 2014). The point I am making, then, is that for Afro-Ecuadorians, the passage of the official or national stance from "monocultural mestizaje" to "multiculturalism" has not been accompanied by the transformations that the change of vocabulary might suggest. Instead, it has re-inscribed the prevalent racial order in a "new" narration of the nation (Bhabha, 1990): Ecuadorian multiculturalism constructs society as composed of a growing and dominant homogeneous majority (the mestizos) that faces a number of small resilient minorities, which often occupy the margins of national territory, and which are organized in distinct communities with their own cultures. These "small" minorities must be "understood, accepted and basically left alone – since their differences are compatible with the hegemonic culture – in order for the society to have harmonious relations" (Anthias and Yuval-Davis, 1992: 158; *El Comercio*, 2004). In Ecuador, since the 1990s, the "small minorities" – mostly the Indigenous movement and the communities of Afrodescendants – have become important or visible political agents.

In passing, I also make the case that unlike what was going

on during monocultural mestizaje, when ideological mestizaje was the only national narrative that could be heard, the present situation is in fact characterized by daily confrontations among various narrations of the nation: mestizaje is not alone anymore in the ideological arena. These conflicting narratives are grounded in different definitions of what the national community is; they also emphasize the difficulty of bringing about the unity of the nation by pointing to the unsettled nature of multiculturalism.

My discussion follows the work of Barnor Hesse (1999, 2000) when he differentiates between the "multicultural" and "multiculturalism" (see also Hall, 2000), where the latter refers to particular discourses and social forms that attempt to incorporate visible cultural differences and distinct ethnicities into one single national formation – in that sense, "multiculturalism can be named, valued, celebrated, and repudiated from many different political perspectives" (Hesse, 2000: 2); and where the former, the *multicultural*, is constitutive of that political configuration and is a signifier of the unsettled meanings of cultural differences in relation to multiculturalism. In this conceptual framework, multiculturalism is the attempt to fix the meaning of cultural differences in national imaginaries. The multicultural is therefore always embedded in a context characterized by a dichotomy between the West and the Non-West, the global north and the global south, the "civilized" and the "savage", which shapes the cross-cultural processes that establish the meanings of the often (if not always) racially marked instances of contested cultural differences. The multicultural is thus central to the transnational processes that diaspora formations constitute and which deeply unsettle the idea of self-contained, culturally independent and self-sufficient nationalist identities. The multicultural also involves – always – processes of cultural entanglements often called creolization (Rahier, 2013, 2014), which question the notion that national forms are coherent and tidy. Thus, the dynamic of the multicultural is to unsettle supposedly well established modern societies through processes of what Hesse calls "transruption", which bring multiculturalism into contested political focus:

> A multicultural transruption is constituted by the recurrent expo-
> sure of discrepancies in the post-colonial settlement. *It comprises*
> *any series of contestatory cultural and theoretical interventions*
> *which, in their impact as cultural differences, unsettle social norms*
> *and threaten to dismantle hegemonic concepts and practices.* Tran-
> sruptions transcend or overcome any initiative to dismiss their

relevance, and continually slice through, cut across and disarticulate the logic of discourses that seek to repress, trivialize or silence them. In the absence of effective or satisfactory resolutions, multicultural transruptions are simply recurrent (*author's emphasis*; Hesse, 2000: 17).

In this article, the best example of transruption is perhaps the case referred to by Saída below, when she shares with the reader the rallying of members of Afro-Ecuadorian women organizations in front of an advertisement for a brand of rum they found offensive because of its depiction of the racialized body of an objectified black woman. Such actions by black activists disrupt the multiculturalist myth about the Ecuadorian nation-state.

When looked at within this theoretical setting, liberal and neoliberal multiculturalism appears as a re-inscription of the hegemonic social and racial ordering of things which existed before its advent, and which is now formulated in a somewhat different political configuration with the help of a "new" vocabulary. Charles Hale (2002, 2004, 2005, 2006) emphasizes the links between neoliberal economic reforms and multiculturalism in Central America. His remarks are pertinent for Andean South America, particularly when he affirms that neoliberal governance has included a

limited recognition of cultural rights, the strengthening of civil society, and [the] endorsement of the principle of intercultural equality. When combined with neoliberal economic policies, these progressive measures have unexpected effects, including a deepened state capacity to shape and neutralize political opposition, and a remaking of racial hierarchies across the region (Hale, 2005: 10)

STEREOTYPES ABOUT BLACK BODIES AND BLACK SEXUALITY

Stereotypes about blackness, black bodies, and black sexuality in particular abound in Ecuador. These stereotypes share many similarities with comparable representations of blackness in other national contexts, or on the transnational scene. Of note is the enduring stereotype that constructs black women as hypersexual beings and that has had devastating consequences on the lives of Ecuadorian black people, and on Afro-Ecuadorian women in particular (Rahier, 2014).

This research follows the work of a variety of scholars who consider the connections between power and sexuality to be important because the relation that we have with ourselves as sexual beings is a fundamental component of modern identity. Giddens (1992: 15) discloses for example: "Somehow… sexuality functions as a malleable feature of self, a prime connecting point between body, self-identity, and social norms." And before that, Foucault (1978: 103) had already stated: "Sexuality is not the most intractable element in power relations, but rather one of those endowed with the greatest instrumentality, useful for the greatest number of maneuvers and capable of serving as a point of support, as a linchpin, for the most varied strategies."

Franz Fanon's *Black Skin, White Masks* (1967), although problematic because of its characteristic peripheral treatment of black women, has been conceptually fundamental to this work. For Fanon, sex and sexuality are not exclusively about personal or individual pleasures and desires. He approached sexual desires and sexual practices or performances as being highly responsive to social and historical circumstances. Where others – such as Freud (Diana Fuss, 1995; Lévi-Strauss, 1962; Merleau-Ponty, 1962) – have theorized about the body in such a way as to standardize the white male body as the norm based on which all other bodies had to be evaluated and imagined, Fanon powerfully introduces the notion of the (non-white male) racialized body, the black body, which is, he asserts, in colonial and "postcolonial" (neocolonial) contexts, an ontological impossibility (see also Mohanram, 1999). Where the former studies reproduced the Western tradition that consists in "disembodying" the white male by standardizing his body, Fanon insisted upon the opposite: the "embodiment of blackness" or the fact that blackness is not but body.

> Though he focuses on the dimension of racial subjectivity, his analysis of the individual is always rooted in the larger socio-economic, material framework of colonialism. *Black Skin, White Masks* effects, then, a paradigm shift that reconfigures psychoanalysis to account for racial identity and that enables a psychoanalytic critique of racism (Bergner, 1995: 10-11).

The expansion of Europe in non-European spaces came along with the otherization of "non-European" peoples and their transformation, from a eurocentric perspective, into "inferior races". Indeed, since the beginning of the eighteenth century, European imperialist discourses of "otherization" of non-European peoples very often used sexuality as a trope. In these discourses, sexuality is manipulated in two different ways. References to sexuality serve either to construct brown and black peoples as savage-like individuals whose character is denoted by "immoral", "abnormal" and "obsessive" sexual practices or, by contrast, sexuality appears as the very metaphor of the imperial enterprises where white males conquer foreign and faraway lands that are symbolized by available brown and black female bodies waiting to be penetrated.

Irvin Schick (1999) writes of "ethnopornography", the nineteenth and most of the twentieth centuries' anthropological or ethnographic discourse on Oriental sexuality, as well as some literary works that were nothing but "an instrument of the exercise of geopolitical power". In many of these texts – particularly literary texts – foreign lands, which Schick calls "xenotopia", are profoundly sexualized; and we find in them abundant brown and black women – the "omnisexual Others" – who appear as symbols of the lands to be conquered by the white men. As Foucault (1978: 32) notes, "Discourses on sex did not multiply apart from or against power, but in the very space and as the means of its exercise." In these discursive constructions of "non-Euro-American Others" through the theorizing about their sexuality, the stereotyping of black or Sub-Saharan women's sexuality has been quite edifying. This stereotyping must of course be understood in light of the contrast they make with the moral norms surrounding white women's "purity", bodies, and sexuality that first emerged in the eighteenth century. black and brown women's bodies and sexuality have been construed in direct opposition to the way white European women's bodies and sexuality were imagined or reported, idealized and standardized as norms for proper female bodily characteristics and behaviours. We can recall here, for instance, the work of Sander Gilman (1985a, 1985b) on the tragedy of Sartje Baartman, the so-called Hottentot Venus, and the obsession of European medical doctors of the eighteenth and nineteenth centuries for her vagina lips, and especially for her "vaginal apron"; and for her buttocks, which were compared to the same body parts of Italian prostitutes (abnormal or pathological white women), before reaching conclusions about the naturally enormous sexual appetite of black women in general:

> What gave European forms of prejudices their special force in history, with devastating consequences for the actual lives of countless millions and expressed ideologically in full-blown Eurocentric racism, was not some trans-historical process of onto-logical obsession and falsity – some gathering of unique force in domains of discourse – but quite specifically, the power of colonial capitalism, which then gave rise to other sorts of powers (Ahmad, 1992: 184).

BLACKNESS AND ECUADORIAN NATIONAL IDENTITY: *SEÑORAS* AND *MUJERES*

The statements above briefly present known information about "transnational", Eurocentric, and racist, stereotypic representations of black women's bodies and sexuality. Although many of the representations under scrutiny here do share similarities with representations reproduced in other national contexts – at least in the Americas and in Europe – every national context does indeed present a series of circumstantial particularities related to specific socioeconomic and political processes and histories that make of each one of them and their attendant racialized oppressions a singular story that needs to be approached with respect to its uniqueness (Hall, 1992: 12-13).

To comprehend the situation of Ecuador, one must keep in mind that black women's femininity and sexuality in that specific historical context have been imagined and ideologically constructed in direct relation, if not definitive opposition, to the femininity and sexuality of two other categories of females: the white females (including so-called white-mestizo females), and the indigenous females. For the purpose of this discussion, we could limit the ideological landscape of Ecuadorian femininities to a simplified situation where we have, without mentioning masculinities for now, three fundamental actors: white (and white-mestiza) females, indigenous females, and black or Afro-Ecuadorian females. In this article as well, I have some use for the two fundamental socio-cultural categories – racially informed – that are also at work in other Latin American and Caribbean contexts (Brettell, 1995; Douglass, 1992; Melhuus and Stølen, 1996; Ulysse, 1999): the categories of "lady" or *señora* on the one hand, and "woman" or *mujer* on the other.

Emma Cervone (2000) has written on the characteristic masculinity of the Ecuadorian elite's voice and imagination of *mestizaje*. The latter logically leads to the conception of (blonde and blue-eyed) white and white-mestiza females and their sexuality as aesthetically and morally ideal. These ideals constitute more or less violent standards that every woman should try to attain at all costs. This standardization and its attendant construction of "Other bodies" have been encrypted in various aspects of the Ecuadorian landscape: everyday vocabulary and conversations; written and visual representations in the media; texts of songs and popular culture; and literature.

Here is an anecdote that illustrates well this racial ordering at work in the Ecuadorian common-sense. In August 1999, in the plane that was taking me from Miami to Quito, I met an Ecuadorian white-mestizo, an acquaintance of mine whom I had not seen for years. He is an architect who was working at the time in the office of Quito's mayor. He explained that he had been traveling in the U.S. with some of his colleagues to look for funding for one of the mayor's construction projects. It was an evening flight, the plane was half empty, and we had been drinking wine with our dinner. After requesting some more wine from the flight attendant, he asked me why I was going to Ecuador this time. I responded that I was working on a new research project. He wanted more details and I began to explain that the project focused on black women's sexuality in Quito, as well as on the ways the racial order was, or was not, a major factor in the shaping of black people's, and in this specific case, black women's sexuality.

I wanted to go further in my explanation when he suddenly interrupted me to share his views on the matter. Making an abstraction of my own blackness, he went on to theorize that unlike white people and "Indians", black people wherever they are found, failed to repress their sexuality; they had a much freer rapport with their bodies; their sexuality and their natural sensuality were important and normal parts of their daily lives. *"That is why they dance the way they dance, with lascivious body movements; even the way they walk... even the way they walk...."* (he repeated). From watching the facial expression he had at that precise moment, his wine cup in hand, his eyes lost on the ceiling of the plane's cabin, I wondered what he was thinking about, if he was just daydreaming about one of his phantasies. (I know his white-mestiza wife.) For him, this "sexual permissiveness" – as he seemed to suggest – explained the particularity of many of black people's daily behaviours. His authoritative monologue was beginning to irritate me when, thank goodness, one of his colleagues asked him to join their group a few rows away. The relatively quiet violence of his "common-sensical comments" goes to the heart of what I am trying to accomplish in this article.

The examination of the conceptual distinction between "lady" or *señora* and "woman" or *mujer* helps us understand the ideological contrast made, on one side, by white and white-mestiza female bodies and sexuality, and, on the other, by black bodies and sexuality. For the purpose of this article, we could discuss the two concepts this way: A señora, *dama*, or lady will be white or white-mestiza; she will be educated and espouse all the norms of "social respectability"; she will be viewed as being dedicated to having children and will not be associated – in male conversations – with sexual pleasure; her body will be well covered and never exposed in the public space; she will not be employed (until the recent economic crises) and will have at least one maid to take care of her house; she will attend social events in the evening, often accompanied by her husband. Her sexuality is not exposed in the public space. She is "pure" motherhood. She almost seems to have children without engaging in sexual intercourse. Her icon is the Virgin Mary, the Mother of Christ.

By contrast, a *mujer* or "woman" will be black or dark-skinned; she will be thought of as being of easy sexual access to men; she will be uncovering her body in public spaces in "indecent ways"; she will eventually have sets of children with different men; she will be uneducated and employed as a maid or a cook; her mannerism will be said to be "un-refined"; her body shape will be voluptuous, almost conceived as being naturally obscene or vulgar; she will be the occasional lover of white, white-mestizo and white-mulatto married men, who will comment with loquacity in male gatherings on "black women's sexual prowess" and the curves of their body parts with expressions such as *una buena negra* (a good-looking black woman), *una negra caliente* (a hot black woman), or even by referring to specific body parts more explicitly (usually the buttocks and the legs). In contradistinction with the señora, the body of the mujer is often associated with the devil.

It is interesting to note here that just as it has been the case in other Latin American national contexts, twentieth century writers from regions associated with blackness have reproduced these stereotypes about black women's bodies and sexuality in their poems and other works in a way that shows positive intent – as in the case of the Esmeraldian writer, Nelson Estupiñán Bass, in his work *Canto negro por la luz* (1954: 34), among others.

From the perspective of modern, urban Ecuadorian society, Indigenous or "Indian" female bodies and sexuality have been construed as if they exist off to one side of the fundamental opposition described above between white and black females. If in many ways Indigenous females do unequivocally enter into the category of "woman" with the black females, unlike the latter they do not appear in the same position when references to physical attractiveness and exotic sexuality are made. In fact, in the popular iconography, as well as in written texts, Indigenous women very often appear as non-sexual beings who supposedly smell bad, who are submissively working all the time to raise their children, work the fields and sell in the markets, and who often beg at the traffic lights with their most recently born child tied to their backs. Their bodies are usually represented as unattractively small, and deprived of the curves that characterize black women's bodies in the popular imaginary. (An exception should be made here about Indigenous women from Otavalo and their changing representations.)[1]

This relative "attractiveness" of the black woman when compared to the similar processes of imagination and cultural construction of the Indigenous female's femininity, body, and sexuality should not be simplistically interpreted as a positive feature within the racial order because, as Lola Young (1999: 81) observes:

> For the black women who have been deemed beautiful and objec-tified by a white masculinist gaze, their distance from the white feminine ideal has not produced [an] unambiguous revulsion... rather, it has been a substantial part of their appeal. However, this attraction, based on the exoticism of otherness, is just as prob-lematic as the racism from which it has emerged.

Let us now focus on the impact these stereotypes have had on the sexual life histories of four black female Quito residents.

FRAGMENTS OF FOUR NARRATIVES
OF BLACK FEMALE SEXUALITY

Dominant stereotypical representations led the first woman (Salomé) – who was born in Quito – to become obsessed with her virginity, as well as to obtain and preserve a reputation of being a (respectable) *señora*. Throughout the years, since her teens, she literally developed a phobia (the term she used) of being penetrated and has been unable to shed that fear until relatively recently. Two of the other women, María and Yesenya, were born in rural areas and migrated to Quito where they ended up as sexual workers.[2] Unlike Salomé, they have been, in a way, "capitalizing" on the popularity of stereotypes of black women's hyper-sexuality by selling their bodies to multiple penetrations by – mostly – white and white-mestizo men. The fourth woman, Saída, graduated from a university in Ibarra, the capital of Imbabura Province. She lives in Quito where she is employed and self-identifies as a political activist who is engaged in the plight of Afro-Ecuadorians.

Salomé

Salomé[3] (S): I was an attractive adolescent. They called me *rompe corazones*, 'heart breaker'. There were quite a few white and white-mestizo boys chasing after me, because I was born and I grew up among white-mestizos in Quito. Until adolescence I didn't really have black friends. The only black people around me were my relatives, but they lived far away, in the [Chota] Valley. When walking in unknown white-mestizo neighborhoods, I suffered racist aggression. If I crossed the street where some white-mestizo male kids were hanging out, they immediately shouted things like *negra rica* ('delicious or attractive black woman', 'how attractive this black woman is'), and things like that. Very often, they would pay particular attention to the curves of black women's legs and their behind and say: 'That black woman has a nice butt!' I was able to understand that what they were saying was not simply complimentary, but on the contrary was profoundly disrespectful. That is when I became conscious of my condition as a black woman and as a sexual object. They have so many tales about the fact that men can cure illnesses by having sex with black women – like to cure kidney diseases. They say that black women have a lot of sexual energy and that they can go on and on. I realized that what they were really after was my body, they just wanted to have sex with me. It would be quite strange, in fact, to see a white or white-mestizo Ecuadorian man wanting to be with a black woman as a partner for life (*Excerpt from a 1997 recorded conversation*).

I met Salomé for the first time in 1996, during a party organized in Quito by a friend we had in common. Thanks to the financial help of her older brother, who was then single and who was working as a government employee, she graduated from a local university with the equivalent of a Bachelor of Arts degree. She worked for a foreign NGO until about 2010. She was born in Quito from working class parents who migrated from the Chota-Mira Valley. We progressively became good friends and we would meet on numerous occasions I visited the country. Puzzled by her insistence to claim a *quiteño* background, I began the very first of a series of interviews in the late 1990s and early 2000s by asking her to share with me the way she conceived her black identity, how she identified as a "black *quiteña*" and what that meant vis-à-vis the so-called traditional black communities, and particularly in relation to the community of the Chota-Mira Valley. I was used to spending time with Afro-Ecuadorian political activists who often visited Afro-Esmeraldian and Afro-*Choteño* villages, who reproduced a discourse about black identity in which rural black communities appeared as the source of "authentic blackness" and Afro-Ecuadorian traditions. I was, then, surprised by the negative tone she adopted when referring to rural Ecuadorian blacks, whom she saw as being somehow inferior to her and to the other more educated, urban, young blacks in general. She said:

Salomé (S): That's a fact, we are Afro-Ecuadorians. Our roots are in Africa. That's where our ancestors came from.... But, at the same time, there are two groups here in Ecuador that are located in a specific region: Esmeraldas and the Chota Valley. I do not identify with any of these two groups! Because I grew up in another space, I grew up in another environment, with other customs, with another worldview, and fundamentally with the objective of realizing my full potential [*superarme*], with the desire of becoming better, with the commitment of showing to the world that black people can also be important. Unfortunately, there is a consensus out there that black people from Ecuador do not like to work. Many Ecuadorian blacks accept life with the little they have. They are not very ambitious.

Jean Muteba Rahier (JMR): It seems that you have a lot of negative feelings towards the people of the Valley.

S: It's very simple. I wasn't born in that environment. Therefore, I cannot say that I identify with that group. Because, there is a tradition out there that wants us, the black people, to always identify as a unified and homogenous group. It's a fact: I was born in another space, in another environment... I do not feel as a part of that group. I do not identify with the people of the Valley, or of Esmeraldas. I identify as an Ecuadorian! I feel Ecuadorian, and I like to be an Ecuadorian. It infuriates me that people do not believe... or accept that I am from Quito. Why is it that if you're black you automatically must be from Chota or from Esmeraldas?

Although she recognizes the existence of racism, which she says she has experienced since the age of 10 or 12, she nevertheless claims that most of the negative ideas about black people in Ecuador (see Rahier, 2014), and particularly the negative images of black women, are justified. Let's listen to her again:

S: It is very hard to feel racism, when young white and white-mestizo men denigrate you in the streets or segregate you just because you're black. It hurts. But I think that the people who act that way do so because they are ignorant, they don't know any better. But, I think that these racist things are also happening because of the people of my race. Because, we have to acknowledge that what they say is true. Although we are a relatively small portion of the Ecuadorian population, the number of black men who are involved in delinquent acts is quite high. black people have always been seen as violent and dangerous people. Even myself, as a black woman, I am sometimes afraid to get too close to them, particularly when I am alone. On the basis of my personal experience, I cannot say that it's a lie that black people are lazy, that they don't do a thing, and that they only think about leisure, that they are vulgar and disrespectful, that one has to be afraid of them. It is true because I have lived it. Unfortunately, because of the bad economic situation of the country, the majority of the sexual workers are indeed black women.

JMR: The majority?

S: Yes, I think that it's the majority. That's what I was able to observe in the streets of the city. Perhaps it's not the majority, but at least many of them are. Of course, there are many social and cultural reasons that have brought people to characterize black women as women who are preoccupied by sexual satisfaction. Unfortunately, they don't say this or that other woman. They simply say 'black women'! And this is not true! And all of us, black women, we suffer from these images. Usually, when I wait for the bus in the street, it does not matter if I have a skirt that goes from the belt down to my shoes, white and white-mestizo men approach me and ask how much I charge for sexual services. They think that all black women are prostitutes or potential prostitutes who have children like rabbits, one after the other, from adolescence on.

Salomé has clearly been profoundly impacted by the racist, stereotypical representations of black people in Ecuadorian society to the point where she obviously contradicts herself. On the one hand, she accepts the stereotypical representations at face value and reaffirms their validity, while on the other hand she wants to insist that not all black women fit the unfair stereotype.

She explained how for her, sexuality – and especially sexual penetration – has always been something very special, very unique that she wished to reserve for the man who would be her partner for life. She also explained that she had several boyfriends (mostly whites and white-mestizos) with whom she always refused to give the so called *última prueba del amor* (the ultimate proof of love) – that is to say, to allow vaginal penetration. She always kept in mind that she needed to educate herself, that she would not have children before finishing her education and before finding the right man with whom to build a family. She explained, referring to specific experiences she had, that in fact she did not like either Afro-Ecuadorian men or Ecuadorian white and white-mestizo men because of their *machista* ways and their lack of respect for women in general, and particularly for black women. She explained how she had grown up preferring European and North American men because, she said, they are more respectful of black women than Ecuadorian men are. She thinks that they have more respect for blacks because in Europe and North America, it is normal to find respectable black women and men in a middle-class position, as professionals. She sees me as a good example of that. She stated how hurtful the depreciative comments of white and white-mestizo ladies about black females are.

She also explained that she had reached her thirty-second birthday without losing her virginity thanks to the practice of masturbation and also because she had developed, along with a "clitoridian sexuality" (the expression she used), a real "phobia for penetration" (her own expression) that I cannot help but relate to her aspirations for respectability. As she herself puts it:

S: First, being a virgin, I always thought of sexual intercourse as something very special, healthy, as something that is not dirty. On the contrary, I think about it as something very special that one shares with somebody special. I think of clitoridian masturbation in the same way, as a search, an encounter with one's own body. Because if to scratch your nose when you have been bit by an insect gives you personal satisfaction, why not do it with the rest of your body? And all that crap about the fact that masturbation is a sin, I don't believe in it. I have masturbated since the beginning of my sexual awareness. Sometimes I masturbate a lot. I think that it is the most natural way to let off the steam of one's own sexual energy without needing the presence of a man.

About her phobia about being penetrated, she said:

S: I discovered that something was wrong with me, that each time I wanted to offer my body for penetration, I was invaded by a tremendous panic, like a trauma, a phobia for penetration. I was invaded by the sensation that I was going to be badly damaged. And sometimes, I even wished that it would be good in a way if one day someone would rape me, so that the fear that was in my head would go away.

Then she referred to specific occasions when she had tried to "give the ultimate proof of love" to a European boyfriend, and was – at the very last moment – unable to let it happen. She emotionally explained how much that "phobia" had hurt her and made the possibility of a stable relationship with a man unreachable. She expressed feelings of inadequacy in her womanhood. In fact, through the years, she developed a big cyst around her uterus. Its growing size progressively provoked unbearable pain to the point where she decided to visit medical doctors. The two gynecologists who examined her diagnosed a psycho-somatic ailment, and expressed their surprise at seeing a woman of her age who was still a virgin. For more than a year, she tried to avoid the cost of a surgical operation by visiting traditional healers or *curanderos*, to no avail. Her cyst was surgically removed in 1999. A year after the operation, she literally forced herself to lose her virginity with the young French man with whom she was involved at the time, without telling him anything about her condition. To her great surprise – as she says – she did not feel anything: no pain, no pleasure! This feeling continued during the following penetrations she experienced with him. This lack of vaginal pleasure has been for her a great disillusion:

S: For me, I had had orgasms at the level of the clitoris, but I've never had a similar or comparable explosion as the result of a penetration, and that has been quite frustrating. I know that we women are very different from one another. But I didn't expect to be a woman who is exclusively clitoridian, who doesn't get pleasure from vaginal penetration. I was left with a profound deception.

Salomé now lives in Cumbaya, a suburb of Quito, in a house she has shared with her German partner for more than 20 years. Because she couldn't have children, they adopted a young Afro-Esmeraldian boy.

María

After listening to the story of Salomé, amazed by what I interpreted as the profound impact of the racial-spatial order, I decided to work on narratives of sexual history from Ecuadorian black women living in Quito. The obsession of Salomé with respectability, and her will to prove that she does not fit the stereotypes of black women's sexuality, led me to try to gather similar information from black women involved in sexual work, because I thought that their relationship to these stereotypes would provide good material for comparison. I expected them to be directly inverted to Salomé's relationship with the same stereotypes.

I met María thanks to a friend, a white-mestiza woman who, as a social worker, had been involved with the Association of Sexual Workers of the Province of Pichincha. She introduced me to the president of the association who put me in contact with María,[4] one of their black members.

María was born in Quito from a black woman from the Chota-Mira Valley and from a white-mestizo father, whom she never met. She thinks that her father must have been the last employer of her mother in Quito. Indeed, not long after María's birth, her mother moved from Quito to Ibarra to take on another job as a domestic employee. In 1999, her mother, who was 60 years old, was still a domestic employee in a white-mestizo home of Ibarra.

At the moment of our interactions in 1999, María was 38 years old. She did not finish primary school and married very early – both legally and ecclesiastically – a black man from the Chota-Mira Valley. They lived in Ibarra and had six children. Her husband was abusive and often drank. He sometimes beat her up. One day, because she refused to give him money she had earned herself, he burned all of her clothes. That was when she decided to leave him. She went to Quito with her children. Life in Quito was a struggle for her. Looking for a place to live, she found a big room (four brick walls with a zinc roof on top) that was to be used by the night guard (*guachimán*) of a garage. After negotiations, the garage owner allowed her to use the space free of charge in exchange for taking care of the place after hours; she just had to pay for the electricity and the water (she still lives there). She had different jobs as a domestic employee.

> María (M): Yes, where I was working before, I experienced racism. Racism is strong in Quito. People say things like: 'dirty nigger!' and 'lazy nigger'. When I worked in a family of rich people, they were sometimes saying *negra de mierda*, 'shitty nigger', but not to my face, behind my back, and I was hearing it. But I was making out as if I hadn't heard it. But once I reacted and lost my job. This was when I was working in the house of (white-mestizo) people living in the González Suarez (an exclusive street with expensive high-rise apartment buildings in Quito).

One day, while on the bus on her way to work, she overheard a conversation between two other women (one black, and one white-mestiza). One of them was explaining to the other that she had engaged in sexual work, that it was not so bad because the money came in everyday in greater quantity than with any other job one could think of. The money one could make had no comparison with the salary of a domestic employee. After hearing that conversation, she decided to work as a sexual worker. She has been doing so in three different neighbourhood bar-brothels on the 24 de Mayo Avenue since 1995. Situated in the south of Quito, this neighbourhood is known for its cheaper prostitution.

M: When I began working, the price of one sexual intercourse (*una ficha*) was 7,000 *sucres* (in 1995).... Then I went to another bar because I had problems with the owner of the first one. In that second bar, I was making between a hundred and two hundred thousand sucres a week. To get that, one had to make three, four or five fichas a day; it was the equivalent of 20 to 30 thousand sucres per day. This was not bad at all at the time. Today (1999), one *ficha* is 25,000 sucres (one U.S. dollar in 2000), with one beer. The people who come to the clubs where I have been working are workers (*trabajadores*); they are not executives. The people with more money go in the clubs of the north of the city (see below).[5]

She is proud to say that she has been working in the bar where I first met her, *El Paraíso de Mujeres* (Paradise of Women) for more than three years. Having Salomé's story in mind, I asked her what she thought of the stereotypes about black women's sexuality: if they had been hurtful to her – and if so, how. She enthusiastically responded, with a touch of pride:

M: They say that black women are hot, that they are hotter than white women, or white-mestizo women. They are hotter and they can satisfy men. They can have sex without getting tired of it; they have a good sexual appetite. I'm like that, and my 'husband'[6] became used to me and my sexual appetite; and he is *blanco* but he cannot get enough (*el es incansable*). We are the same, that is why we get along well in sex. We are good friends.

Talking about her condition as a black sex worker working mostly among mestizo and white-mestizo colleagues and clients, she indicated that black sex workers who work in the same bar usually stick together: there are always fights among women during which, whatever the initial problem was, "race" becomes very quickly the principal issue. As she explained:

M: There are [mestizo and white-mestizo] clients who prefer to be with a black woman. In my case, I'm not in a rush, I'm not demanding them to go fast to finish, and they prefer me because I take my time and I do it well. I want them to talk well about me, so that they come back and make me a good reputation. I have my clients. I identify as a black woman. I have black blood and this will be like that until I die. I have had black clients, African clients. They are nice people. The only thing is that they don't like to talk a lot. They come to do what they want and that's it.

With Yesenya in mind (see below), I asked her if she refused to have sex with black clients.

M: No, not at all. There are black men who prefer white women, there are other black men who prefer mulatto women, that's how it is. I have no problem with black men. Anyway, they are fewer than the mestizos and white-mestizos. There are some white-mestizo colleagues who do not like black men because they say that they have big penises and that they make love for too long, that it hurts, and so on. For me, all men are the same. I don't have this prejudice, but I know that black men have bigger penises, particularly African men. White men have penises of all sizes, many have it small, skinny, long and tiny, but others have a bigger one. But the majority are the same, an erected penis is an erected penis; it will get inside of you as deep as it can, that's all.

Many clients like to go with a black woman to have anal sex, because they say that black women have nice buttocks (*lindas nalgas*). Personally, I don't like anal sex, other women do, not me. To avoid it, I ask a prohibitive price that I know they will not be able to pay. Every woman does what she wants. One day, I'll leave that job. I can sew! I can cook!

Yesenya

Yesenya[7] was born in 1969 in the city of Esmeraldas, from Afro-Esmeraldian parents. She is darker skinned than María. I met her in the exclusive strip-club and brothel of the north of Quito where she works. Seeking to interview a black woman involved in upper scale sex work, I went to her club *El Rincón de Placeres* (Corner of Pleasures) with a white-mestizo male friend of mine. To approach her, I had to behave like any normal client would. I invited her to my table, offered her a drink, and engaged in a conversation. To be able to keep her at my table for an hour and a half, I had to pay her US$50.00 (around 500,000 sucres in 1999). Although reticent to talk with me at first, she progressively felt at ease and accepted my invitation to meet outside of the club during the day. I visited her home several times after that and met her two "mulatto twins".

When she was two years old, her parents divorced and she went to live with her father in San Lorenzo. Her father was a school teacher. She lived in San Lorenzo until she was 20 years old. After graduating as a *Bachiller* with a [high school] diploma in accounting, she left San Lorenzo due to a conflict with her father's new wife and worked for a while as a secretary in a law office in Santo Domingo de los Tsáshilas, where she met the man who became her husband and the twins' father. Asked to talk about her youth and the stereotypes of black women's sexuality, she said:

Yesenya (Y): When I was not a prostitute, before I got married, as a high school student, I had to go to the library. I wore short skirts and wherever I walked, cars would beep and people talked to me as if I were a prostitute. This has happened to me in various places in Ecuador. Ecuador is a backward country when you consider the issue of racism against blacks. They think that because one is black one has to be at the bottom, as if we were still in the colonial period, as if we were still slaves of white people. When I was younger, I was very attractive and a lot of men were interested in me. I had to go out without my mother knowing my whereabouts. She absolutely wanted me to finish my studies and not be distracted. I didn't make love with the men; we just kissed. We caressed one another but without doing anything more. When they asked for *la prueba del amor*, I rejected them saying that they were not serious.

She was a virgin when she met the man who was to become her husband. He took her virginity by raping her:

Y: He was born in Ecuador, from Australian parents. He has the face of a *gringo*, and his eyes have a nice honey color, just like gringos have. His hair is light brown and his skin very white. He was a traveling salesman of electro-domestic equipment. He passed by Santo Domingo a lot. When I first made love, it was with him, although we were not married at the time. We went on a trip to Quito. We stayed in a hotel after dinner, in a room with two beds – one for me and one for him. At midnight, while I was sleeping, he came into my bed and, although he knew that I was a virgin, he penetrated me at once. I screamed because I was sleeping. It was horrible! I'm a very good sleeper, but my body was hurting so much. When I went to the bathroom, it was painful to walk, it was horrible. Aïe! I don't want to remember this. He apologized. I slapped him several times. Then we went back to Santo Domingo. He said that he wanted to live with me, and that he loved me. I told him that if he really wanted to do that, we had to get married. He accepted and we got married. This marriage was more for my dignity and not so much for love. Then, we had the twins. I lived with him for 8 years.

She described her life in Santo Domingo. He continued to travel for his business and returned as often as he could; he was very jealous. She did not have to work and even had a domestic employee for almost two years (a black woman from the Chota

Valley). Her husband became increasingly jealous. He was 24 years older than she was. At one point, his jealousy got out of control and he began to lock her up in their house. She revolted and had a big fight with him. They later solved the conflict by moving to Quito, where she also was a housewife receiving the help of a domestic employee. Her husband was often drunk, sometimes for entire three-day periods. One night, two years after the birth of the twins, while drunk, he flew into a violent burst of jealousy and threatened her with a big kitchen knife. "That's when I told him that I would never see him again, and until this day I haven't", she said.

She left her house with her twins and her sister, who was living with them at the time. They went through tough times for a while. At first, they found refuge in the house of an Esmeraldian friend who was also living in Quito. The first job she found was as a cook in a restaurant.

Y: When I got my first paycheck, it was only 500,000 sucres. I bought milk for my children and then I rented a room. Almost all of the money was gone. We all went there. We spent the first night on the floor covered with newspapers and towels. A friend of mine took my children. Her name is Alicia. She let the kids sleep in her bed while she slept on the floor. Alicia is from Ibarra. She is black as well.

Then she left the restaurant. She was ashamed to work there as a cook after having lived in many ways the life of a lady for years. She enlisted in an agency for temporary work, but they only wanted to give her jobs as a domestic employee.

Y: Here, to be able to be an accountant, I had to show my documents. They did not recognize my diploma from San Lorenzo. They wanted me to take computing classes. In Ecuador, if you are black, they won't let you live like they let the whites live. All of that because you're black! That's why Ecuador is a mediocre country, because of racism. It will never get better!

She then worked as a domestic employee in the house of a white-mestizo medical doctor for a few weeks.

Y: Everything was going fine until the doctor began to look at me as a woman and not as an employee. He was talking to me in the ear. He was taking me by the waist and saying things such as: 'Let me tell you, you are quite attractive!' When his wife wasn't there, he wanted to go to Ibarra with me. He was very much after me all the time. He was saying that I was suggesting sexuality just by being looked at. One day, he wanted me to work during the weekend and I went very well dressed. I also wanted to go well dressed because I very much liked a guy from the Galápagos who was living in Quito and I was hoping that he would see me. I wore a mini-skirt. The doctor saw me dressed that way and told me that he would love to rent an apartment for me. That is when I decided to leave that job.

A few days later she was approached in the street by a middle-aged white mestizo man who lured her into becoming, as he said, a masseuse in a spa for older people. He said that the beginning salary was very good (700,000 sucres monthly) and would increase according to her performances. She quickly found out that his expectations were not for her to be a masseuse; he wanted her to be a prostitute. At first, feeling cheated and disappointed, she thought of running away from the place, but the need for money made her stay. Yesenya had been a sexual worker in three different exclusive bar-brothels in the north of Quito during the two years preceding our meeting. These bars are exclusive because of the high entrance fee as well as the high cost of their sex workers. The clients who frequent them – Ecuadorian white and white-mestizo professionals, and foreign businessmen – can easily spend the amount of the legal minimum salary (around 120,000 sucres in 1999) in one night. The women who work there are younger and generally have a better physical presence than the women who work in the south of the city. The bars are well kept and luxurious in comparison to the Paradise of Women where María works. During the course of a night of work, every woman must strip on stage several times. Clients choose the woman they like and either bring her to one of the equipped rooms on the second floor of the club, or pay an extra fee and leave the club with her. Yesenya told me that on a good night, she goes home with almost US$200.00. When she works, she leaves the kids in the care of an older white-mestiza neighbor, whom she pays a monthly salary. Because of the relative financial affluence of the clients who go to her bar, Yesenya has had access to a kind of "relationship" unknown to María: Clients sometimes hire her to spend a few days with them on the beach, or for the duration of a cruise in the Galápagos Islands, or another vacation destination. When this occurs, a kind of romance may develop between the client and her, and the story always ends up with some financial gain. She says that she fell in love with her client on two of these occasions.

Paralleling Salomé's story, numerous sections of Yesenya's narrative denote a similar tortured relationship with blackness.

For example, when talking about her first flirts with men, before meeting her husband, she related an episode with a young black man from San Lorenzo.

Y: One day, before meeting my husband, I went to San Lorenzo where I met an old 'love'. One of these flirts that I was talking about earlier. He was black, very dark. He was beautiful, but then I said to myself: 'I am black and I will marry a black man? Why would I do such a thing? We will get very dark kids, and I don't want to do that. I want to improve my race (*Quiero mejorar mi raza*).'

JMR: So you think that the black race is bad?

Y: No, not bad, but I'm very dark. If I were to marry him, our kids would be very dark too, and this is ugly. I didn't marry him, but I loved him because he never asked me to have sexual intercourse. That's why I liked him. My color is beautiful, but just for me, not for my kids. My kids are beautiful, they are of your color [she points towards me] and they have 'good hair' (slightly curly hair). I'm proud of being black but not for my kids. I don't take black kids in my arms. I don't like them. When my friend (a dark skinned black woman) comes to visit, I don't let her touch the hair of my kids, because I don't want to take the risk that she could hurt (*dañar*) my kids' hair just by touching it. When they were little, my kids had straight hair and one day I made the mistake of cutting their hair very short. When the hair grew back, it became curlier, while it was entirely straight before. That is when I began thinking that I didn't want anybody with kinky hair to touch their hair. I don't want my kids to have such 'nappy' hair. I'm very careful with the shampoo I choose.

I never had a sexual/love affair with a black man, never! black clients, I had only one, a 'black gringo' from Haiti. He was very dark, like Johnny Ventura.[8] I didn't want to go to bed with him, but he offered me very good money and we had sex. He made love to me something like five or six times. At one point I told him that my vagina was beginning to hurt, that I wanted some peace now, that he had a big penis, that he should stop. He treated me as a prostitute and not as a woman one has seduced. After that I decided that I would never again go to bed with a black man. My clients are always white, either Ecuadorians or gringos. I like to have white clients, particularly gringos, because they pay well. I also like white clients because they are not too demanding (*fastidiosos*) in bed. They do not have too much sexual appetite. There are also white men who have difficulties sustaining an erection. I also like the gringos because they like to go to fine places for dinner. They invite me to travel in the country.

The difference between a black client and a white one is this:

White guys want to be with a black woman because they never penetrated one before, and they want to have the experience. Also, the body of a black woman is very attractive. So, sometimes, they even say that they want to be well treated for their first time with a black woman. They say that black women have a particular flavor, that sex with them is better. They just say it. They say that white women are not passionate enough (*son apagadas*), that they go to bed just passively, waiting for the man to do everything. The black woman, on the contrary, is more active. They say that black women have a smaller and tighter vagina, and that their vagina is warmer, that their skin is soft, like the skin of a baby. White men like to caress the skin of black women in a way that black men don't, because black men also have this kind of skin. White men even fall asleep caressing one. I love to be celebrated, and white clients do that. The Gringos, when they go to a club, they look directly for a black woman, and if there are no black women, they go away. This is not all gringos, of course, but most of them seem to like black women a lot; but the white and white-mestizo guys from here, the *longos* (pejorative word for *indio* and depreciative term for 'mestizo'), they like black women to discover them, to find out how they make love, to caress their curves, because we have nice bodies. Very few white women have nice bodies. They have flat behinds, not like black women who have nice, round behinds. black women, we are hotter, we know how to make love in a more exciting way than white women.

Saída

Saída[9] was born in Quito in 1970 from Afro-Choteño parents. Her mother was visiting relatives in Quito at the end of her pregnancy. Saída is the last one of her mother's six children. Shortly after her birth, they moved to the Chota Valley, where they lived until she became of age to attend primary school. She went to primary and secondary school as well as to college in Ibarra, where she lived with her mother. They visited the Valley almost every weekend and every holiday, particularly when it was harvest season. Although she physically spent a lot of time in Ibarra, she always kept in contact with the Valley and grew up in Afro-Choteño environments. She obtained the equivalent of a Bachelor's degree in Teacher Education in natural sciences from Ibarra's Universidad del Norte. After graduating, she worked for a while in a kindergarten in Ibarra. She has been residing in Quito since 1997 after finding a job with a politician from Imbabura province who was involved in national politics. She had met that politician in Ibarra a few years earlier. She worked for more than a year in the National Congress and then found a job in a local university where as a member of staff she is charged with the responsiblity of seeking funding from national and international organizations to conduct development projects in rural black communities aimed at educating community leaders, and to help young people enroll in high schools and colleges. When I asked her how she identifies as a black woman now that she lives in Quito, her response was:

> Saída (S): You're right, there are young black people who think that the black folks who live in the city constitute one group and that the black folks who live in the countryside constitute another. I think otherwise. It's obvious that we who live in the city have more opportunities. But that does not mean that black people who live in rural areas should be looked at as inferior; on the contrary. In the workshop in which I work, we always invite [black] rural community leaders. We look at them as important social actors. We try to make sure that they have good self-esteem. For me, there is no such thing as rural blacks as separate from urban blacks. We are one black community. You know, when women from the Chota Valley are selling their products at the market in Quito, they look away from me when I go there during my lunch hour, because I have a uniform. A uniform indicates that I've been to school and that I have a relatively good job in comparison to them. They look away and avoid acknowledging my presence as if they felt it a shame to still be selling their products in the market. So, I'm the one who calls their attention by saying, 'Hey, how are you doing? Why aren't you saying hi to me?' and so on, just to demonstrate to them that it's not because one has a title that one is different. We are all blacks and we are all brothers and sisters. And the ones among us who are higher up socially must help the others.
>
> When people ask me where I'm from, I never say that I'm from Quito, although I was born in Quito; I always say that I'm from the Valley. I say that because that is how I feel! I'm not from Quito!

Various sections of our conversations were focused on Ecuadorian anti-black racism, and particularly on racist stereotypical representations of black female bodies and sexuality. She explained that she mostly experienced racism while in Quito, much more so than when she was living in Ibarra, where racism was more subtle, more hidden. In Congress, she was the assistant to a very visible Congressman. On more than one occasion during meetings she attended with him, other Congressmen addressed her as if she were a servant, asking her, for example, to go find some coffee, or bring some food. This happened despite the fact that she was dressed professionally, like other people in the room. Her response indicating that she was not there to serve coffee always provoked the biggest surprise. About the stereotypical representations of black females' bodies and sexuality, she said:

S: Obviously, and that is sad to say, we black women in Ecuador are looked at as sexual objects. At first they look at your figure, your body. Well, we must also say that in general, we black women have a voluptuous figure (*una figura carnadita*) – a small waist, long legs, and round buttocks. That is something that is true. Even the white-mestiza women, not only the white-mestizo men, are amazed by the body of black women. They even say 'Wow, you have a beautiful body, I would love to be like that!' That's what some of them have told me. But when men look at you, you understand right away that they are undressing you and imagining you with them in bed.

White-mestizo men look at you differently than do black men. They look at you as if a black woman is valued only for sex. With black men, it's different. Even if they think you are pretty and attractive, they don't objectify you the same way. Because it's normal for a man to appreciate a woman who has a good body. But white-mestizos go directly to the sexual thing; they say things like: *Que buena es esta negra para los riñones* (this black woman is good for the kidneys). I like to dress with tight clothes, but I don't do it often, because if I do I would be the target of vulgar comments in the street. When you get on the bus, as a black woman, you must be careful with the bus employees who sell the tickets, because they will grab your behind, shamelessly; they'll even feel under your skirt. I have no problem with people telling a black woman that she is pretty, but there are ways of saying it. Many just say it while looking insistently at her buttocks. That is when you feel like a sexual object.

On various occasions, Saída was approached in the street by white-mestizo men who addressed her as if she were a sex worker. She explained how surprised and hurt she felt the first time it happened; she was so amazed by it that she didn't know how or what to respond. Now, when somebody wants to ask anything in the street, she just walks away without paying any attention.

Saída also told me about one of her white-mestiza co-workers who seems to be obsessed by her buttocks:

S: There is a white-metiza at work whom I have asked a thousand times to stop touching my butt. One day I asked her if she liked women. And she responded no, that she is married, that my buttocks just amaze her. She must be around 35 years old; she is thin, and she has no butt whatsoever; she is as flat as one can be. When I dress with pants, she comes and asks me if I put some cushions to augment the volume of my buttocks. Finally, I told her that if she wants to do so she can admire them, but from afar, without touching them. One day, she even told me that if she had a body like mine she would have a lot of men at her feet. I responded that a woman is much more than just a pair of buttocks. But then, she said that the first thing men look at is that, the body. And there, she's right.

Saída explained that she is member of the Pichincha Province black women's association. One day, various members of the association organized a small rally in front of a big billboard, which consisted of a huge photograph of a nude, very dark, black woman with a voluptuous body, and with particularly meaty buttocks. It was an advertisement for a brand of rum called "Ron Negrita".[10] The face of the black woman was not visible. The most important body parts for the advertisers were obviously her back and her buttocks: she appeared naked lying on her right side, viewed from the back, her buttocks visible. The caption of the poster said *El Placer Líquido con la Cola Negra* (Liquid Pleasure [rum] with the Black Tail [the advertised brand]) – the sexual play of words unequivocally suggesting that the "black tail", which stands for "black behind" but also for dark soda (*cola negra*), does provoke "liquid pleasure" (ejaculation) – *Rhum* and *cola* being one of the most popular mixed drinks there is in Ecuador.

A delegation from the association went to the managers of the company that produced the rum, and demanded that the billboard be taken down immediately because it deprecated and objectified black women. The managers promised to take it down, but the display remained. The association's response was to invite the public and the press to witness the staining of the image. The police intervened without arresting anyone, and the billboard was taken down two days later.

Here is some of what Saída had to say about her sexual life experience:

S: I didn't have a boyfriend until I was in the tenth grade. With him, almost three years into our relationship, I lost my virginity. It took a long time [three years] because we were often separated. He was studying in Quito and I was studying in Ibarra. He is from the village of El Chota. He is the father of my son. We met at a festival in the Valley. When I was younger I did not like to hang out with men, and I don't know why. I didn't trust them. I met him first at the wedding of one of my cousins. He was tall, handsome. I approached him; I was 14 or 15 years old. My body was already formed. That night, we almost didn't talk. Then I saw him another time, almost a year later, at a festival of Bomba music,[11] in the Valley. I approached him and told him that I liked him, and I hugged and kissed him. And that is how we became boyfriend and girlfriend. He was four years older than me. For him I also was his first girlfriend. He was studying medicine in Quito. At that time I wasn't that curious about sex. My curiosity began following conversations I had with white-mestiza classmates in high school. From experience, I can tell you that white-mestizas have much more sexual experience than black girls and black women. I think they begin doing things earlier than we do. They were my age but they already had four or five boyfriends, some of them had two or three boyfriends at the same time; they had sexual intercourse with their boyfriends. They were the ones telling me: 'Saída, you don't know what you are missing out on! You are wasting your time!' I was telling them that I was afraid, that I didn't want to become pregnant. They were telling me that sexual intercourse was so nice, that it was marvellous, that it was better than eating the dish you most prefer. These conversations awoke my curiosity about sex. I am the one who asked my boyfriend to have sexual intercourse. At first, he rejected my requests, saying that I was too young, that it would come in due time. He was such a nice guy. Finally, because of my insistence, he told me that we would make love after I graduated from high school. When graduation day came, I made him remember what he had said. And that is how we made love for the first time the day after my graduation. I basically discovered sexuality with him. We had a very nice relationship. Four years after having made love for the first time, I got pregnant. At that time he was living in Ibarra because he was an intern in a hospital there. But after my son was born, we had to separate because he began courting other women, and I didn't like that. He is very much involved in the education of our son.

After that I had another boyfriend; he was black. With him nothing really happened. It was a short relationship. The fact that the father of my son had betrayed me made me even more distrustful of men than I was before.

Then I had another boyfriend who was white-mestizo. That was when I was living in Quito. He was from Ibarra. In fact, because his father was working in the sugar mill of Tababuela (located in the Chota Valley), he was living with his parents in the village of El Chota. He could dance very well. He asked me if I wanted to be his girlfriend and I agreed. But we didn't have sexual intercourse. He respected me very much. Our relationship lasted only three months. When people saw us in the street, hand in hand, particularly black men, they were always asking if there weren't enough black men out there for me to be with a white-mestizo, and things like that. That was a little difficult. He treated me in a very nice way, in a way that black men don't treat you. He held the door open for me, pulled the chair out for me to sit down, took my coat at restaurants. He made me feel like a queen. One day I went to his apartment in Quito and he cooked for me. At one point, we began kissing and caressing one another, and that is when he told me, for the first time: 'Saída, your body drives me crazy!' I immediately got out of his embrace, stood up and asked him straightforwardly: 'Why is my body driving you crazy?' He responded that it was because my body was beautiful and that since he was a healthy man, he was attracted by it.

For me, as soon as somebody talks to me, even in positive terms, about my body, I become distrustful. I don't know why. Perhaps it's because of what white and white-mestizo people always tell you in the streets, I don't know.

Our conversations ended with Saída explaining that she had had sexual intercourse only with one man: the father of her son; that since the end of their relationship she had some sort of a blockage with men; that even in the cases when she felt confident with a man and wanted to have sexual intercourse with him, because she loved him and was very much attracted to him, she was unable to let it happen. She became invaded by the fear of being used only for the attractiveness of her body and not loved for who she was, above and beyond her body. She added that once, in the recent past, she met a U.S. born African American student who was studying in Ecuador for a year, that they were very much attracted to each other, but that the relationship didn't go anywhere because of her incapacity to relate to her sexual self without anxiety. They never made love and the relationship ended. She ended the last conversation we had by confiding in me that she will probably consult a therapist about that soon.

CONCLUDING REMARKS

These narratives show that stereotypical representations of black females as hyper-sexualized beings have had quite an impact on the lives of the four women interviewed, on their self-perceptions, self-identifications, and in the shaping of their sexualities.

Quito, as one of the centers of white and white-mestizo-ness within the Ecuadorian racial-spatial order, manifests virulent stereotypes and anti-black racism. Each one of the four narratives presented uncovers an individual's specific and original trajectory within the racial-spatial order; the greatest contrast appears perhaps between Salomé and Saída: the two black professional women. While Salomé absolutely wants to identify with the "white-mestizo Quito" and disassociate herself from rural blacks, whom she looks down upon, Saída embraces her membership in a trans-local black community in which urban and rural blacks act side by side, actively engaged in black solidarity and political activism.

These narrative fragments indicate that other factors such as class, gender relations in Ecuadorian society, heteronormativity and religion have played a role in the way each one of the four women has shaped and negotiated her identity and her sexuality. Undeniably, none of them would be able to escape from the pervasive white and white-mestizo imagination of black bodies and black sexuality. The constitution of Salomé's, María's, Yesenya's and Saída's subjectivities has not taken place in a vacuum, but within a societal context characterized by a white and white-mestizo hegemony that constructs blacks as Others in part through the circulation of a racist discourse about their sexuality and about the alterity of their bodies. As shown here, this discourse has been imposed upon them more or less violently. As Foucault (1978) suggests, we must understand power as forming the subject, because power provides the condition of the subject's existence and the path followed by its desire. Judith Butler paraphrases Foucault when she writes about the "psychic life of power":

> As a form of power, subjection is paradoxical. To be dominated by a power external to oneself is a familiar and agonizing form power takes. To find, however, that what 'one' is, one's very formation as a subject, is in some sense dependent upon that very power is quite another.... Power is not simply what we oppose but also, in a strong sense, what we depend on for our existence and what we harbor and preserve in the beings that we are.... Power that at first appears as external, pressed upon the subject, pressing the subject into subordination, assumes a psychic form that constitutes the subject's self-identity (Butler, 1997: 1-3).

Although on one hand Salomé, María, Yesenya and Saída all oppose, in different ways, the racist stereotypes and the discursive construction of black women as sexual and moral Others, on the other hand they reproduce some aspects of these stereotypes in a positive light, internalizing the perspective of the powerful in their self-constructions and self-presentations. To resist the "embodiment" of blackness denounced by Fanon (we are not just body; we are more than just a pair of buttocks; black women can be respectable and professionals; what do you mean when you say that I have an attractive body?), we can juxtapose the presentation of the black female body in terms of physical and even moral superiority (in Saída's narrative) vis-à-vis the white and white-mestiza female body and morality (black women have nicer and more attractive bodies; we have round buttocks and theirs are flat like a table; our skin is smooth and pleasant to touch; white and white-mestiza young females are more promiscuous than black young females). Statements about black women's bodily aesthetic superiority sometimes include the reproduction of racist stereotypes about black women's sexuality. That is what we can see in María's and Yesenya's – the two sex workers – narratives: "We black women, we make love better, in a more exciting way, and longer than these *apagadas* (dull) white-mestizas."

In passing, these narratives also belittle the manly-hood of the powerful: the white and white-mestizo male sexual power is inferiorized (they have smaller penises and some of them have difficulty maintaining erections; they are not *fastidiosos*); although they appear as more gentlemanly than blacks, particularly if they come from North America or Europe. The trace of power is found as well in Salomé's and Yesenya's problematic relationship to blackness, and the self-hatred that emanates from their narratives. Salomé ambiguously reproduces as valid the stereotypes that affirm the delinquency of black men and the hypersexuality of black women, without hiding her preference for white European men; while Yesenya finds black kids ugly and black men sexual brutes, despite the fact the she was raped by an almond-eyed white Ecuadorian of Australian origin. She aspires to "improve her race".

Salomé's and Saída's narratives unambiguously demonstrate how difficult it is for young black professional women who do not follow the paths that lead to domesticity and sexual work, to negotiate a space for themselves in Quito.

A similar study conducted in another non-Andean locality, in another national context, in Salvador de Bahia in North-Eastern Brazil or in New York City in the United States, for instance, would surely provide data that differ or contrast with those presented here. Anti-black racism in Quito and anti-black racism in Salvador or New York City, although they all share the same transnational general mechanisms and processes, take different shapes and have different impacts, in light of local histories and processes. However, it is safe to say that all forms of anti-black racism have a direct impact on all aspects, including the most intimate, of the lives of those categorized as "blacks".

---

*This article is reproduced with permission of the author. It was first published as book chapter "Stereotypes of hypersexuality and the embodiment of blackness: Some narratives of female sexuality in Quito, Ecuador" (pp.147-174) in Jean Muteba Rahier's *Blackness in the Andes: Ethnographic Vignettes of Cultural Politics in the Time of Multiculturalism* – © Jean Muteba Rahier 2014.

Notes

1   About the emergence of an Otavaleña middle class, see de la Torre (1996); Colloredo-Mansfeld (1999).

2   One of them refuses to use what she sees as the politically correct term "sexual worker" to refer to herself (see below).

3   Salomé is not her real name. Aware of my intention to publish this material, she asked me to call her Salomé, the name her mother would have loved to call her.

4   María is the name I have decided to give her so that her identity is concealed. I have also invented the name of her place of work, *El Paraíso de Mujeres* (Paradise of Women).

5   Soon after the year 2000, the American dollar was adopted as Ecuador's currency.

6   Her partner, a mestizo man, lives with her and her children. He works as a doorman at *El Paraíso de Mujeres*. That is where they met.

7   Yesenya is the name I have decided to give her so that her identity is concealed. I have also changed the name of her place of work to *El Rincón de Placeres* (Corner of Pleasures). Yesenya prefers to be called a "prostitute". She does not like to be called a "sex worker" (*trabajadora sexual*) because this is the self-descriptive expression used by the (cheaper) women from the south of Quito, such as María. Women involved in sex work in the north of Quito tend to look down on the women who work in the south of the city.

8   Johnny Ventura is a Dominican merengue singer quite famous in Latin America and the Caribbean.

9   Saída is not her real name. I do not reveal her exact place of work in Quito to better conceal her identity.

10 The term *negrita* is a condescending diminutive for "black woman" or *negra*, just like its male corresponding expression *negrito*. The very name of the brand of rhum, therefore, is already offensive.

11 Traditional music of the Chota-Mira Valley.

References

Ahmad, Aijaz. 1992. *In Theory: Classes, Nations, Literatures*. London and New York: Verso.

Anthias, F., and N. Yuval-Davis 1992. *Racialized Boundaries*. London: Routledge.

Bergner, G. 1995. Who is that masked woman? or, the role of gender in Fanon's *Black Skin, White Masks*. *Publications of the Modern Language Association of America* 110(1):75-88.

Bhabha, Homi. 1990. Introduction: Narrating the nation. In *Nation and Narration*, ed. H. Bhabha, 1–7. London: Routledge.

Brettell, Caroline. 1995. *We Have Already Cried Many Tears: The Stories of Three Portuguese Migrant Women*. Prospect Heights, Illinois: Waveland Press.

Butler, Judith.1997. *The Psychic Life of Power*. Stanford: Stanford University Press.

Cervone, Emma. 2000. Machos, mestizos and Ecuadorians: The ideology of mestizaje and the construction of Ecuadorian national identity. Latin American Studies Association Meeting, Miami, Florida. Not published.

Clark, Kim, and Marc Becker, eds. 2007. *Highland Indians and the State in Modern Ecuador*. Pittsburgh, PA: University of Pittsburgh Press.

Colloredo-Mansfeld, Rudi. 1999. *The Native Leisure Class: Consumption and Cultural Creativity in the Andes*. Chicago: University of Chicago Press.

Comercio, El. 2004. Los afroquiteños e indios quieren mayor apertura. *El Comercio*, September 15 (electronic document http://www.elcomercio.com accessed April 12, 2007).

de la Torre, Carlos. 1996. *El racismo en Ecuador: Experiencias de los Indios de la clase media*. Quito: Centro Andino de Acción Popular.

Douglass, L. 1992. *The Power of Sentiment: Love, Hierarchy and the Jamaican Family Elite*. Boulder: Westview Press.

Espinosa Apolo, Manuel. 2003. *Mestizaje, cholificación y blanqueamiento en Quito: Primera mitad del siglo XX*. Quito: Universidad Andina Simón Bolivar, Ediciones Abya-Yala, Corporación Editora Nacional.

Estupiñan Bass, Nelson. 1983. *Cuando los Guayacanes Florecían*. Quito: El Conejo.

Fanon, Franz. 1967. *Black Skin, White Masks*. New York: Grove Press.

Foucault, Michel. 1975. *Surveiller et punir: Naissance de la prison*. Paris: Gallimard.

Foucault, Michel. 1978. *The History of Sexuality*. New York: Pantheon Books.

Fuss, Diana. 1995. *Identification Papers*. New York and London: Routledge.

Giddens, Anthony. 1992. *The Transformation of Intimacy: Sexuality, Love, and Eroticism in Modern Societies*. Stanford, California: Stanford University Press.

Gilman, Sander. 1985a. Black bodies, white bodies: Toward an iconography of female sexuality in late nineteenth-century art, medicine, and literature. *Critical Inquiry* 12:204-242.

Gilman, Sander. 1985b. *Difference and Pathology: Stereotypes of Sexuality, Race, and Madness*. Ithaca, NY: Cornell University Press.

Hale, Charles. 2002. Does multiculturalism menace? Governance, cultural rights and the politics of identity in Guatemala. *Journal of Latin American Studies* 34(3):485-524.

Hale, Charles. 2004. Rethinking indigenous politics in the era of the "*indio permitido"*. *NACLA Report on the Americas* 38(2):16-20.

Hale, Charles. 2005. Neoliberal multiculturalism: The remaking of cultural rights and racial dominance in Central America. *Political and Legal Anthropology Review* 28(1):10-28.

Hale, Charles. 2006. *Más que un Indio: Racial Ambivalence and Neoliberal Multiculturalism in Guatemala*. Santa Fé, N.M.: School of American Research.

Hall, Stuart. 1992. The Question of Cultural Identity. In *Modernity and its Futures*, ed. Stuart Hall, David Held and Tony McGrew, 112-134. Cambridge: Polity Press in association with the Open University.

Hesse, Barnor. 1999. It's Your World: Discrepant Multiculturalisms. In *New Ethnicities, Old Racism*, ed. P. Cohen, 205–225. London: Zed Books.

Hesse, Barnor. 2000. Introduction: Un/Settled Multiculturalisms. In *Un/ Settled Multiculturalisms: Diasporas, Entanglements, Transruptions*, ed. B. Hesse, 1–30. London: Zed Books.

Ibarra Dávila, Alexia. 2002. *Estrategias del mestizaje: Quito a finales del siglo XVIII*. Quito, Ecuador: Abya-Yala.

Lévi-Strauss, Claude. 1962. *La pensée sauvage*. Paris: Plon.

Melhuus, Marit, and Kristi A. Stølen, eds. 1996. *Machos, Mistresses, and Madonnas: Contesting the Power of Latin American Gender Imagery*. London: Verso.

Merleau-Ponty, Maurice. 1962. *Phenomenology of Perception*. New York: Humanities Press.

Mohanram, Radikha. 1999. *Black Body: Women, Colonialism, and Space*. Minneapolis: University of Minnesota Press.

Muratorio, Blanca. 1994. Nación, identidad y etnicidad: Imágenes de los Indios Ecuatorianos y sus imagineros a fines del siglo XIX. En *Imágenes e imagineros: Representaciones de los indígenas ecuatorianos, siglos XIX y XX*, ed. B. Muratorio, 109-196. Quito, Ecuador: FLACSO-Sede Ecuador.

Polo, Rafael. 2002. *Los intelectuales y la narrativa mestiza en el Ecuador*. Quito: Universidad Andina Simón Bolivar, Ediciones Abya-Yala, Corporación Editora nacional.

Rahier, Jean Muteba. 2013. *Kings for Three Days: The Play of Race and Gender in an Afro-Ecuadorian Festival*. Urbana: University of Illinois Press.

Rahier, Jean Muteba. 2014. *Blackness in the Andes: Ethnographic Vignettes of Cultural Politics in the Time of Multiculturalism*. New York: Palgrave Macmillan.

Schick, Irvin. 1999. *The Erotic Margin: Sexuality and Spatiality in Alteritist Discourse*. London: Verso.

Silva, Erika. 1995. *Los mitos de la ecuatorianidad: Ensayo sobre la identidad nacional*. Quito: Abya-Yala.

Stutzman, Ronald. 1981. El mestizaje: An all-inclusive ideology of exclusion. In *Cultural Transformations and Ethnicity in Modern Ecuador*, ed. N. Whitten. Urbana: University of Illinois Press.

Ulysse, Gina. 1999. Uptown ladies and downtown women: Female representations of class and color in Jamaica. In *Representations of Blackness and the Performance of Identities*, ed. J. M. Rahier, 147-172. Westport, CT: Bergin & Garvey.

Wade, Peter. 1993. *Blackness and Race Mixture. The Dynamics of Racial Identity in Colombia.* Baltimore: Johns Hopkins University Press.

Whitten, Norman. 2003. Symbolic inversion, the topology of "el mestizaje" and the spaces of "las razas" in Ecuador. *Jounal of Latin American Anthropology* 8(1):52-85.

Whitten, Norman, ed. 1981. *Cultural Transformations and Ethnicity in Modern Ecuador.* Urbana, Chicago, and London: University of Illinois Press.

Whitten, Norman, Dorothea Scott Whitten, and Alfonso Chango. 2003. Return of the Yumbo: The caminata from Amazonia to Andean Quito. In *Millennial Ecuador: Critical Essays on Cultural Transformations and Social Dynamics*, ed. N. Whitten, 184-215. Iowa City: University of Iowa Press.

Young, Lola. 1999. Racializing femininity. In *Women's Bodies: Discipline and Transgression*, ed. J. Arthurs and J. Grimshaw, 67-90. London and New York: Cassell.

THE POLITICS OF BLACK HAIR

A Focus on Natural vs Relaxed Hair for African-Caribbean Women

MICHAEL BARNETT

Abstract In this article the author attempts to discern, through consideration of past literature and collected ethnographic data, factors that influence African-Caribbean women to alter their natural hair – chemically or otherwise. A key premise that frequently cropped up was that the underlying motivation for them to straighten their hair was an embedded sense of shame of their natural hair. In other words, they rejected their natural African hair as a result of internalized self-hate. Another reason that surfaced from the study was that of economic security: The sentiment that black women are more employable with relaxed hair as opposed to natural hair still exists. Yet another reason was based in tradition: Perming one's hair has come to be seen as something that black girls do automatically to mark their transition from childhood to adulthood, and not following suit would result in many being deemed outcasts.

Key words • Natural hair • Relaxed hair • Self-hate • Tradition • Economic security

IDEAZ Vol. 14 • 2016 • ISSN 0799-1401 (69–100)
© Centre for Tourism & Policy Research / Ian Boxill – UWI, Mona

This article discusses race and its attendant standards of beauty in Jamaica in a context where not only is one's shade or complexion considered important, but so too is the texture of one's hair. Along these lines, while there exists a plethora of material on skin bleaching, the same cannot be said about attitudes to hair texture among black women (particularly as far as the anglophone Caribbean is concerned). In this regard this article intends to tip the scales (albeit in a small way) in the direction of balance.

An ethnographic approach was employed in obtaining data for this article, wherein a number of semi-structured interviews were conducted among several black female respondents, along with the sifting of data from specially organized forums on the topic of attitudes towards hair in Jamaica.

A key premise that crops up frequently when it comes to the topic of stylization of black women's hair, is that in many cases the underlying motivation for black women to straighten their hair is due to a deep-seated desire to distance themselves from their natural "kinky" hair. In other words, many black women seek to reject their natural black features and emulate white physical characteristics as a result of self-hate based on the internalization of a white supremacist worldview and the racialized hierarchies associated with this. Writers such as Eramus (1997), Fanon (2008), Miller (1969), Nehusi (2002), and Tafari-Ama (2006) are just a handful who have articulated this relatively popular perspective that the internalization of white hegemonic beauty ideals can create a sense of shame of one's own natural features.

The reasoning behind the "internalized white supremacy" perspective is basically as follows: Along with the ideology of white supremacy comes the notion of black inferiority. Hence it is by no means a leap of the imagination to posit that the development of low self-esteem among blacks results from their internalization of white supremacy. Fanon (2008) speaks emphatically of the wide-ranging impact that the internalization of white supremacy has had on blacks, not just in terms of the way they interact with whites, but in the way they act towards each other.

Writers such as Nehusi (2002) and Tafari-Ama (2006) argue that the extremely lucrative black hair and skin bleaching industry stems largely from a deeply ingrained inferiority complex among blacks. Tafari-Ama (2016) affirms that the twin practices of skin bleaching and hair straightening are present-day indicators of the internalization of racialized notions of embodied aesthetics that are white defined and are designed to reproduce white supremacist narratives of power and self-identity politics. She goes further to assert that as a consequence of the compromised self-image/self-concept of the black woman there have evolved many multi-billion dollar industries of hair and skin products, laced with chemicals, that target women of colour, who have already been duped through institutionalized narratives of identity representation that reify "European looks" as the benchmark of social and sexual desirability.

The internalized shame that historically has been associated with black hair in its natural state started from during slavery days, according to Byrd and Tharps (2014). A common practice of

Europeans during the enslavement process of Africans from the West Coast of Africa was to shave the head of both the male and the female. It was in a fundamental way the start of a process of stripping them of their individuality, their culture and their identity (Byrd and Tharps, 2014). Also, of course, just as in contemporary times, forcibly shaving the heads of the slaves served to break their spirit, and made them easier to control. Once on the plantation, the female slaves were worked so hard that they did not have the time to braid their hair in elaborate hairstyles (as they had done prior to being enslaved). As a result, they resorted to wearing rags or scarfs over their heads, not only to hide their undone and uncombed hair, but also to hide things like ringworm that sometimes developed in the distinctly unfriendly environment in which they had to work. In contrast, those women who worked in the "big house" (house slaves) had the time to attend to their hair, and were also afforded the opportunity to wear wigs, just as did their male and female masters (Byrd and Tharps, 2014).

In the early 1800s slave ships stopped coming from Africa, because of the outlawing of the transshipment of slaves by England (1807) and America (1808). For one thing, this meant that slaves in America could no longer be worked so hard, as their lives were now worth more. As a result, they started getting Sundays off. That gave women time to do their hair – which they would still cover in a rag during the week but uncover on Sundays for church (Byrd and Tharps, 2014).

So far as hairstyling was concerned, however, things did not go back to the way they had been in Africa for at least two reasons: First, there was a lack of hair care products – no one in America sold palm oil or the right kind of combs; black women had to make do with butter and bacon grease and in some extreme cases, black men used the axle grease for carriages on their hair to give it a straighter look. In terms of combing implements, the carding combs for sheep were used in many instances. Second, after living so long in a country where white supremacy was the norm, black women internalized the notions of black inferiority, which led them to embrace the concepts of "good hair" and "bad hair" – where kinky hair is seen as "bad hair" and straight, flowing hair as "good hair". As a consequence of this, they tried to straighten their hair even if it meant using dangerous chemicals like lye, which they mixed with potato, vaseline, and soap at times to create a formula known as "conk" (Byrd and Tharps, 2014).

The idea of good hair was further strengthened by how house slaves often looked: Many were half white or near white, which meant they often had what was considered to be "good hair". After the civil war, when the slaves were freed, the idea of "good hair" grew stronger – as the blacks who had been freed before the war wanted to hang on to their position at the top of black society and used as their justification the notion that light skin and "good hair" made them superior (Byrd and Tharps, 2014).

This was the context in which a contrast between natural and straight (relaxed) hair developed during the course of the 1800s (Rooks, 1996). As early as the 1830s the selling of haircare products for blacks was commonplace in African American periodicals in the U.S. North (as were beauty parlours run by free African American women). These early advertisements focused on products to lighten the skin and straighten the hair. Simultaneously, however, there existed "black pride" discourses that advocated for an imagery that would counteract the arguably damaging representations promoted by the advertisements (Rooks, 1996: 35).

During the late 1800s African American intellectuals and middle class men championed black hair in its natural state as the preferred style. This trend became even more apparent in the early twentieth century, during and after World War I, when activists such as Marcus Garvey, W.E.B. Du Bois and J.A. Rogers advocated that blacks, especially women, embrace what they deemed to be a natural and inherent beauty born of one's African heritage. Contrastingly, black female entrepreneurs such as Madame C.J. Walker exploited the desire of black women to straighten their hair through creative innovations. In the case of Madame C.J. Walker, it was the hot comb (Rooks, 1996: 49).

Tate (2009) presents various perspectives on the factors that determine how black women choose to wear their hair. In chapter 2 of her book she outlines what she terms the "anti-racist aesthetic" perspective on black hair. Essentially she argues this perspective valorizes and celebrates "dark skin" and "natural afro-hair" (2009:39), and is motivated by the realization that in the wider world there exists a hegemonic beauty ideal – one which idolizes white standards of beauty and simultaneously devalues what are commonly recognized as African physical features. Tate (2009) commendably notes that the Rastafari movement, which hails from Jamaica, is an example of a group that strongly adheres to the "anti-racist aesthetic" perspective. The movement unapologetically strives to de-center the iconity of beauty, which it considers to be based on a white ideal, by embracing African hair in its natural texture and praising dark skin and African features in general (such as full lips and a broad nose).

Notably, Tate (2009) does not consider self-hatred to be the only factor that influences black women to straighten their hair. She argues that in some cases it is simply an alternative way or choice for black women to wear their hair. Donaldson (2012) shares a similar line of thought. For one thing, she argues that to consider all hair straightening practices for black women as a manifestation of self-hate is an oversimplification that fails to take into account other possible factors such as the need to assure economic security, or the practice of following a cultural script or tradition (considered by this author to be thoughtful additions to the self-hate perspective). Another factor Donaldson (2012) attributes to the practice of hair straightening is the impact of the media on black women's psyche (i.e. being unknowingly brainwashed by various media). Further, Donaldson (2012) cites a factor that seems to be articulated often by black women with straightened hair (Banks, 2000; McLean, 2015), namely, that it provides scope for a more manageable hair grooming and hair care routine (a perspective that this author finds to be somewhat debatable).

HAIR STRAIGHTENING AS A MEANS TO AIDING ECONOMIC SECURITY AND ASSIMILATION

In regard to economic security as a contributing factor to hair straightening for black women, a strong case can be made for Jamaica as well as the U.S. In a February 28, 2012 *Gleaner* article by Janet Silvera entitled "Policewomen fight to wear Afrocentric hairdos", we are informed that at that point in time the only natural hairstyles allowed for police women serving within the Jamaican Constabulary Force were fine corn or cane rows. Other natural hair styles such as twists, Chinese or Nubian bumps, dreadlocks or fat plaits were not allowed. In contrast, texturized or permed (creamed) hair was perfectly acceptable. This is just one example of the sort of discrimination levelled against natural black hair for black women in Jamaica in some professions.

Commendably, Donaldson (2012) links the economic security factor with that of assimilation. She argues that black women use hair straightening as an assimilation mechanism based on a belief that it conveyed a non-threatening image to white and mainstream society and allowed one to more easily blend in with the rest of society. In Chris Rock's documentary *Good Hair* (2009), actress Raven-Symone relates her understanding of hair straightening as a way to blend in and make those unfamiliar with black hair (especially whites) more comfortable. In her words, "Relaxing one's hair is a way to make everybody around you more relaxed."

Extending the assimilation concept leads to the notion of black women not only straightening their hair to make everybody around them feel more relaxed, but to make themselves as marketable as possible on the job market. According to Abdullah (1998) and Thompson (2009), black women with natural hair in many cases are deemed unkempt, unprofessional and downright unemployable. Byrd and Tharps (2014) detail a highly publicized incident in which 37-year-old Hyatt Regency Hotel cashier Cheryl Tatum was fired in 1988 for refusing to take out her braided hairstyle. Her supervisor called the hairstyle "extreme and unusual". If, by contrast, Tatum had worn her hair straightened it would have been very unlikely that she would have been fired at all. Donaldson (2012) notes that the decision to conform to a dominant style of beauty or to go natural may just come down to a choice between economic security and destitution.

HAIR STRAIGHTENING AS PART OF TRADITION OR CULTURE

Another reason that black women indulge in the practice of hair straightening might be attributed to tradition. Donaldson (2012) again aptly observes that the practice can be seen as part of a cultural script that black women are encouraged to follow. In other words, for black women straightening their hair is part of a group standard. Banks (2000) argues that hair straightening has become such an integral part of the black female identity that it is generally done automatically without much thought put into it. Hair straightening has become the norm, while leaving it in its natural state is the aberration. Along with the normalization of the practice of hair straightening, there is the constant media bombardment of particular images of beauty as well as the constant hair "valuations" from one's peers that all go to reinforce the practice. In essence, then, a key motivation for hair straightening is the adherence to a strict cultural norm that is still present in black communities across the globe.

HAIR STRAIGHTENING AS A PRODUCT
OF THE PROMOTION OF DOMINANT IMAGES
OF BEAUTY BY THE MEDIA

Notably, women and girls of most cultural groups (not just those from black communities) draw upon images in the media to shape their definition of beauty. With the notable absence of celebrity role models and images of women with kinky or natural hair in advertisements and in black magazines (as well as mainstream women's magazines), there is space for a subliminal message to be communicated that natural hair is not sexy, fashionable or desirable. The abundance of images of women with long, straight, flowing hair that are promoted in the media only act to encourage black women to straighten their hair in a bid to emulate these popular images. If images of beautiful black women with natural hair continue to be few and far between, it stands to reason that the tendency for many black women to straighten their hair as opposed to keeping it natural will continue and the pressure to conform will be considerable. Banks (2000) sums up the situation beautifully in this author's opinion when she argues that as a result of dominant images of beauty being so heavily internalized, many black women do not see leaving their hair natural as a viable option.

Donaldson (2012) argues that though the influence of media and advertisements on black women is one which encourages them to straighten their hair and emulate white characteristics (at least subliminally) this should not be considered a form of self-hatred, as they are merely emulating what is popular. This author disagrees somewhat with this position, as in his opinion, to the extent that black women actually perceive themselves to be (or buy into the notion that they are) more beautiful with straightened hair, than with their hair in its natural texture, whatever the outside influences maybe, the indication is that at some level they have internalized a social hierarchy for hair texture within a hegemonic framework for beauty. And once one even entertains the thought that their natural state of being is inferior to or less desirable than a chemicalized/processed state of being, one runs the risk of internalizing some degree of an inferiority complex at the very least or a degree of self-loathing of one's natural hair, whether consciously or unconsciously (subliminally).

This author looks at hair from the perspective that even today (well into the first quarter of the 21ˢᵗ century), it is considered to be an essential and indispensable component of a woman's beauty. And, for black women in particular, this age-old adage seems to be particularly resonant. For instance, in Jamaica in 2012, US$7 million worth of wigs and hair weaves was imported – up from US$3.3mn in 2008. Notably, importation of hair products to Jamaica is fourteen times higher than it is to the other Caribbean countries (combined), and exceeds the value of importation of cars from South Korea to the island annually. (In terms of Jamaican dollars and at an exchange rate then of roughly J$100 to US$1, for the first six months of 2013, more than J$600mn was the estimate given for the importation of hair extensions, eyelashes, wigs and other hair related paraphernalia.[1] The implication here is that by the end of 2013 more than J$1bn, or US$10mn, would have been spent on these imports.)

In a May 2011 article published in the on-line newsletter *Madame Noire*, H. Fields Grenee reported that "African American hair and the cultivation of that 'look' via the placement of weave is a multi-billion dollar industry." In that article, Grenee quotes Davarian L. Baldwin, Professor of American Studies at Trinity College, as saying that weave had become a way for more black women to achieve the "good hair" status, even if only synthetically. Baldwin went further to say: "The culture surrounding weaves, such as the links between more traditionally white hair textures and the pricing system of weaves, helps to exacerbate the notion of 'good hair' as 'non-Black'." Notably and very profoundly, he also affirmed that: "In hair weave stores there is certainly a hierarchy of hairs that is also linked to a hierarchy of racial value."

According to Grenee (2011), since 2000 the number of African American women now suffering from anorexia and bulimia has ballooned. He attributes the increase in these eating disorders to these women buying into the mainstream media image of white beauty, which includes "silky long hair and a slender physique which many black women's fuller shapes cannot naturally accomplish".

Nikki Walton, a licensed psychotherapist who practices in North Carolina, told Grenee (2011) that she had recently made the choice to go natural with her hair, and actively counsels African American women on how to do the same. She pointed out that many of her clients "tend to go natural because it's a healthier choice for them. The vast majority are unfamiliar with their hair's real texture, because they've had perms since they were five or eight" (Grenee 2011). She further pointed out that because many black women have internalized the pervasive negative bias against African textured hair (black hair in its natural state), it takes them a while to get used to wearing their hair natural. Her advice to black women as relayed by Grenee was, "Just go out and get comfortable with your hair. Just embrace the anxiety and insecurity because sometimes you have to fake it before you can make it" (Grenee, 2011).

In a Black History Month forum, convened by this author, held at the Mona Campus of the University of the West Indies in February 2013, Dr Donna McFarlane (presently curator and director of Liberty Hall: the Legacy of Marcus Garvey) reflected:

> I remember my daughter telling me that she wanted it [her hair] to smooth down when she came out of the pool like some of the other girls that go to her school. I also know of women who were natural, had beautiful hair, not because of their Christian beliefs but because they wanted to be so. But as they got older and older and couldn't find a man, they creamed their hair. I know two such cases where they cream their hair if they are not married, because for them this was the important thing to do for the men who were looking for women.

So far as this author is concerned, the notion that having "soft (good) hair" as opposed to "coarse (bad) hair" makes one more appealing and physically attractive as a black woman is cause for concern. If we should push this line of thought further, it would seem that for black women to have their hair chemically processed to make it appear straight and long (characteristic of Caucasian women) as opposed to leaving it naturally thick and tightly curled has become the norm. Thus, paradoxically, those black women in Jamaica who choose to wear their hair in its natural and unprocessed form are (even today) seen to be the aberration rather than the norm. They are the de facto deviants, while those with creamed hair are the "standard-bearers". It would appear that the idea of a black woman having her hair natural – whether it be long or short, or even if she were practically bald – is a departure from expected practice. Interestingly enough, and by contrast, if a black woman in the Americas transitions from her natural hair to a texturized/permed hairstyle she is usually met with much approval. In fact, this process can be considered, in every practical sense, "a rite of passage" of sorts, or even "a coming of age" practice for many young Jamaican girls who are just entering their teens.

Some of the testimonials given by young black women at a 2012 Black History month forum[2] convened by the author and entitled "Notions of Beauty in Black Communities Globally" highlighted the trauma that some of them experienced as young girls wearing their hair natural in Jamaica. A member of the audience, Natalie Huie, language communication major at UWI, Mona campus, explained:

> … the first point I wanted to talk about was hair and how hair is viewed. When I was in high school, a couple of times I ventured… I wore my hair like how I wanted to wear it personally… like chiney bumps or in an afro but you see when I went to school, especially when I wore my first chiney bump to school when I was in grade 9… it wasn't the first but it was the first in a really long time and I wore it to school and basically, a teacher pointed out to me that my hairstyle wasn't right that it was 'bathroom'… it was a style you wear to the bathroom or to your bed; but my hair was actually like neat chiney bumps differently but… they pointed out to me that I should go and do something about it. When I was in 6 form, lower 6, I wore it to school and my teacher was saying I should pull it out because it wasn't right; or another time when I wore an afro, I was told to go and catch up my hair. Now, the thing that frustrated me then was, the girl with long straight or curly hair can wear her hair out but like me, the second I step into the school, it's like people are looking out and as soon as they see you, girl, you need to fix that. On a level it's really upsetting as the person who has natural hair – sometimes, cuz you're like 'ok, I can't, I'm not allowed to wear my hairstyle like this….' Another point I'd like to make – Personally, I've been in stores and my hair is kinda like in an afro and somebody would point out to me that I should put my hair up because it might not be 'hygienic' or something like that because my hair is out. But I'm looking at it: other people with straight hair or curly hair, with hair that's long… they can wear their hair out, fine – and nobody says anything. Their hair is flying as well, I'm sure.

Another young black female member of the audience, Leslean Robinson, final-year marketing student at UWI, Mona, remarked:

> I went to a traditional high school. In first form… the reason why my hair is processed, I was in denial until I came here and listened to all of this.I came to this realization why my hair is actually processed. I remembered in first form at a traditional high school, I used to wear my hair in a big pom pom, I loved the pom pom look. It was the easiest thing and my coordinator came to me and told me, 'Young girl you need to tame your hair, it looks like a mop.' And I remember every morning she used to come to my class and look for me to tell

me to plait my hair and I got sick and tired of it that I actually went and processed my hair. That was the realization, that's why I processed my hair. And when I processed my hair, every day, this teacher came to me and said, 'Your hair is so nice, it's so long and it's so thick'; and all the girls came to me... 'Oh, your hair looks so nice, you know.' Now I start getting attention. So you know who mek dem hair remain processed. So that's what I wanted to point out. Thank you.

According to an article written by Davina Henry entitled "Not So Sexy, Naturally – Unprocessed Hair Not Perceived As Sensuous For Female Entertainers" (*The Gleaner*, June 16, 2013), Trudy Ann Campbell of Island Naturals, a newly formed support group for black women with natural hair in Jamaica, stated that the music industry is not keen on women who sport a natural hair look as they are "not very receptive to artistes with natural hair... people are under the impression that natural hair is only associated with Christians and that isn't a hot trend". Nadine Sutherland, a well-known Jamaican female artiste, pointed out in the article that natural hair is usually associated with consciousness and non-sensuality and that it is totally contrary to the Eurocentric and typical appearance of video vixens who sport long, straight hairstyles. It should be noted that a connection of sorts is made between certain genres of music and hair styles in Jamaica. To be specific, while it is acceptable for black women who perform Christian music (gospel) to wear their hair natural (as sensuality or sex appeal is supposed to be played down here), black female artistes who perform dancehall music, (which is very sexual in nature), require a "permed (relaxed) do" to portray sensuality, making the music as well as the female artiste more appealing.

INTERVIEWS WITH NATURAL HAIR SALON OWNERS

Recently there has been a boom in natural hair salons catering to the needs of black women who want to maintain natural hairstyles. Probably the first ever natural hair salon was Back to Eden, founded and conceptualized in London in 1986 by Cynthia (McDonald) Judah, a Rastafari woman, presently residing in London, England. Cynthia remarked to me in an interview back in 2007,

When I first opened my salon back in 1986 very few hairdressers had any idea where to start when it came to locks, and were not really partial to catering to this hairstyle either to be honest. Thus my first customers were Rastafari, which was on reflection some-

Figure 4.1 • Cynthia Judah, Proprietor,
Back to Eden Natural Hair Salon

what paradoxical. I say this because for many devout Rastafari it is taboo for anybody else outside of the individual, other than one's life partner that is, to touch one's locks.

When the interviewer asked Cynthia how she was able to attract Rastafari to her shop given this taboo, she responded:

> Because I was Rasta myself this made a big difference and at that time the emphasis was on nurturing and nourishing the scalp and the locks with homemade concoctions, rather than the grooming of locks. The initial few who came were so pleased with the results that they highly recommended me to their brethren and sistren such that my client base started to grow and grow. On top of that my shop was not only a place where one came to get their locks attended to, it also became a positive space where like-minded people could meet.

As Cynthia further reminisced on the early years of opening her business, she recalled:

> When I first opened my shop in 1986, Rastas were shunned at that time in England, because of the locks. You couldn't even get a menial job as a Rastaman, let alone a decent work. Then all of a sudden in the nineties, wearing locks seemed to become fashionable. I think that Jazzy-B and his group Soul to Soul had a lot to do with popularizing the wearing of locks in England. Now it's not just a Rasta thing. It's become commercial. You have the sister locks now; that's what's getting really popular. The amount of clients that I have now, especially the women – I can barely cope. The demand is so strong in fact that I've opened up another branch of Back to Eden in St. Mary, Jamaica.

So far as the interviewer is aware, Cynthia is now enjoying a distinctly increased client base, with black people in England recognizing her salon Back to Eden as the leading centre for natural African hair.

As we come back to Jamaica, we see that presently there are at least two prominent natural hair salons in the capital, Kingston. These are Beautiful Earth Natural Hair Salon, owned and managed by Dr Veronica Reid, and Jus Natural, Jamaica's first Natural Hair Salon, owned and managed by Princess McLean and Trudy Greenland.

On Friday, January 23, 2015 I interviewed Princess McLean of Jus Natural at the Mona Campus of the University of the West Indies. When I asked her what inspired them to start Jamaica's first ever natural hair salon, Princess replied:

Figure 4.2 • Princess McLean and Trudy Greenland,
Proprietors, Jus Natural Hair Salon

Well, both myself and Trudy had natural hair, and had so for all of
our lives. I am one of Lorna Wainwright's daughters. That is Lorna
Wainwright that operates Tuff Gong Studios on Marcus Garvey
Drive, Downtown Kingston. She raised me and my siblings such
that we all had locks from we were young children. I grew up as a
part of the Ethiopian Orthodox Church here in Jamaica and have
had locks all of my life. So wearing the locks has become part of
who I am. Similarly in the case of Trudy, her father is a deacon
in the Ethiopian Orthodox Church, and she is part of the church
community, so she has had natural hair all of her life. Trudy used
to service clients with natural hair for about five years before
we both founded Jus Natural. At that time though she used to
work from a small rented booth in a regular hair-dresser's shop
on Molynes Road as well as go to some of her clients' houses to
do their hair. In fact for a while Trudy used to visit my house to
do my hair. Then one day I suggested to Trudy that we should
combine resources and open a shop that catered exclusively
to natural hair. At that time (the year 2001), there existed no
exclusively natural hair salons in Jamaica. You had a shop called
Monica's at Half Way Tree, but they didn't do natural hair exclusively. They also did the processed hair thing. So that meant that
the client who was going to the shop to get their natural hair
tended to had to sit beside someone getting their hair processed
and put up with the smell of all the products they were using.
That really wasn't satisfactory. So we recognized that there was

basically no place that natural hair clients could go and get their hair tended to by hairdressers who specialized in natural hair in a comfortable and relaxing environment. As a result I decided to use some money that I had saved from working abroad and put it towards starting a natural hair salon along with Trudy. We ended up renting a space at the Bob Marley Museum at 54 Hope Road and installed all the necessary fittings for a hair salon. That was the birth of Jus Natural. It was 2001 and it was a proud moment.

When asked what gave her and Trudy the confidence that there was a strong enough market to sustain a natural hair salon, Princess remarked:

Well because my mother is Lorna Wainwright, I came to know a lot of people in the music industry. Also both myself and Trudy were members of the Ethiopian Orthodox church. This meant that we knew a lot of people that had locks and natural hair. On top of that because both myself and Trudy wore locks, there were some women who admired our locks and wanted to know where we got our hair done. So we already knew that the market was out there. By this time locks was becoming very popular. Persons wanted to look professional, while they had their locks. We just knew that the market would be there as we figured that there must be people out there that had natural hair and wanted to look good.

In the responses that Princess provided to the interviewer's questions it was clear why there was the immersion in a natural hair culture in her case. Clearly this was due to a cultural upbringing. Although not mentioned by her overtly, it was clear that Rastafari influences played a role. If nothing else, Rastafari is an intrinsic part of the music scene in Jamaica.

The interviewer wanted to know what advice Princess had for black women who insisted on creaming their hair because they felt that it was more manageable, or even that it was more sophisticated worn that way. Her response was very thoughtful:

Well, first of all, I would try to stay away from trying to convince persons to go back natural or maintain their natural hair because when you say that creamed hair is more manageable, in truth that is a fair statement as the hair is now straight so all you have to do is brush it back into one and then go. So it does take a little less work. However, you have to look at the long-term benefits of anything that you are doing (you can't just look at the short-term benefits). Your natural hair is something that you are born with, so you can't compare it to something that you have chemically changed. It's your mindset. If somebody is saying that they are not ready to go back to their natural hair, and that is your attitude, then I would argue that it is harder to eat healthy than it is to go to a fast food restaurant and indulge. But that doesn't mean that it is the right thing to do. Definitely in our society it is clear that the things that are easier are not necessarily the better things to do. Most of the time people will come to that understanding in their own time. Sometimes it is hard to convince someone that the hair that God created on their head is the hair that they should have. If you can't see that, then it is evident that it is something in your mind that has to be changed for you to accept that.

The interviewer probed further: "Do you think that the prevalence of black women who process their hair is due to the internalization of white ideals?" Again, Princess was prudent in her response:

I would say that back in the day, yes! Black women were process-ing their hair because they wanted to be more acceptable towards whites. They sought social mobility. But now it has trickled down to just being a hairstyle. I have friends who have processed their hair and they are very afro-centric, they are very black, their hair just happens to be processed. So I wouldn't say that most black women have straightened hair because they don't love themselves or because they don't believe that they are beautiful. Maybe they just don't know better or maybe it's because when they were growing up... their mother processed their hair from they were young, so they don't even know what their natural hair looks like. Or maybe they think that their natural hair may stop them from getting a job, not because they see their natural hair as intrinsically bad, but because it's what society thinks. So they feel under pressure to conform. Let's say you go for a job in a bank. Maybe you have to process your hair to get that job. Sometimes because of how society is set, people may walk the line. Because not everybody can open up a natural hair salon and not every-body can do a job that will allow them to wear their natural hair in its free state and feel confident that it's not going to stop them from getting that promotion, or that society will accept them in whatever realm of business they are in.

Dr Veronica Reid is both owner and manager of another well-known natural hair salon in Kingston, Beautiful Earth Natural Hair Haven. Dr Reid, who has a PhD in marketing, is a strong advocate for natural hair for black women. In the 2013 Black History month forum,[3] entitled "Hair Stories: Exploring Pervasive Attitudes Towards Hair and Beauty within Black Communities", she introduced Beautiful Earth:

As a haven for natural hair, one of the things that we don't do [in my business place] is we don't bring any of those black hair

Figure 4.3 • Dr Veronica Reid, Proprietor,
Beautiful Earth Natural Hair Haven

magazines because we are talking about representation and as a people who are familiar with what is in these hair magazines, that's not the type of representation I'd like to have in my surroundings. So those are not the kinds of things that we are going to have.

With regard to recruiting stylists for her business, Veronica retorted:

When I employ stylists it doesn't make any sense asking them about their qualifications, because there is no qualification for natural hair [in Jamaica], even with a certificate from HEART. What they teach them is simple. They might learn to cut, they might learn to colour, but in terms of actually caring for African hair, that's not really part of the curriculum. What they're actually taught is how to change our natural hair textures. So they would learn how to cream (relax) hair, how to put it in weaves, how to braid, but in terms of learning how to shampoo natural hair properly, what kind of products to use in African textured hair, you're not going to find that knowledge in people who are going to these schools.

As a result, Veronica has created her own programme in African hair care and trains her staff herself. She opined further at the forum:

In America and on the continent of Africa, you find that a majority of us, I would say, do not know how to care our hair. And so we see where a two-year-old and I mean those young children, the parents are in a sense forced to resorting to relaxing the hair because they don't know what to do, because we are not taught and that again comes from the fact that there's no value that is put on your natural hair that comes out of your scalp. So why would we teach people how to take care of that kind of hair?

Veronica's presentation at the forum was distinctly thought provoking on the issue of whether or not black women who wore wigs or weaves of African hair texture could be considered as having a natural hairstyle. She contended:

When we put up a picture of Kelly Rowland who was sporting a big Afro Puff wig on the Red Carpet, on Facebook, I was thinking – she does look like a natural African ancestry woman, even if technically, that is not her own hair. And so it came to me that maybe the issue is representation and what exactly are you representing with the different kinds of hair that you may wear? So again, a lot of people say, 'Oh I just want to look different' – but everytime you do something to look different, you mean you want to look different from your race and so these are the things that we have to think about.

In wrapping up her presentation at the 2013 Black History month forum, Veronica was unequivocal:

One person on Facebook said being natural is an actual state of mind, once a person with natural African hair understands and celebrates their own physical attributes without all of the tired excuses about why they wear weave, blonde, blah, blah, blah, then the battle is won. As a mother, as an aunt, I would prefer my children, my nieces, my nephews to see African textured hair all around them, even if it's a weave or even if it's a wig. So it's just hair right? Because that's the statement you hear all the time. But I would say wrong! The choices that we make about our hair, our clothes, the way we tend our bodies are connected to our deeply embedded, but mostly invisible perceptions about ourselves, our identities and our place in society at large. When a majority of African ancestry women believe that they have to wear their hair straight in order to succeed, personally and professionally, then we clearly have a problem.

Another interviewee who presented a perspective on natural hair was a young black professional, Cherrie Tulloch. What the interviewer found interesting about Cherrie, was the confidence with which she carried herself – this, further enhanced by

Figure 4.4 • Cherie Tulloch

the pride and grace with which she wore her manicured locks. Cherrie who in fact has a medical degree and is a practising medical doctor was probably one of the most articulate of my respondents. When I asked her why she decided to lock her hair and wear it natural, she replied:

Our culture has subconsciously and systematically rejected the sum total of what makes us beautiful and black. Society has covertly and overtly rejected our defining features – from the dark tones, thick kinky hair and dark brown eyes. Too many of our women seek to capture a sense of beauty through the acquisition of long straight hair, bleached out skin and fake eyelashes, and the list continues. Straight or curly hair is 'good' hair and the excerpt 'anything black nuh good' from Trevor Rhone's *Old Story Time* echoes the unfortunate mindset some of us have. Some hide it under the banner of self- or artistic expression. Some give the excuse that natural hair is too hard to manage. But it is my humble opinion that for some persons all these modifications are simply a cry for affirmation. We have so rejected that part of ourselves that we no longer invest the time to learn how to manage our own hair. Yet we spend countless hours and monthly visits to the hairdresser to make our hair straight or to manage the extensions. Why should anyone feel the need to do all those things to be deemed... beautiful? Why can't being happy with one's natural state and being beautiful coexist?

This response resonated strongly with the author, especially since the popular rationale that African hair is simply not manageable in its natural state has always seemed to him like a convenient excuse. If one values and loves their natural hair, why not invest the time in grooming it. Is it really that unmanageable, especially with the advent of the afro pick, and wide-toothed combs? Other arguments for relaxing one's hair, such as peer pressure, reasons of tradition wherein it becomes a rite of passage for womanhood, or even to be more marketable on the job market where wearing one's hair relaxed can open more doors, are reasons that the author can more easily relate to.

Other notable respondents were Josanne Lochan, a young black woman pursuing a medical degree programme at the University of the West Indies, and Chyna Whyne, another young black woman who is making her mark as an entrepreneur and emerging Reggae and R&B artist in London, England. Both had the distinction of sporting the bald look as their hairstyle – in Josanne's case, due to a strange quirk of fate; and in Chyna Whyne's case it was simply because she just loved the way it looked.

Josanne Lochan was born with partial alopecia – which means that she has been bald all her life. Most people assume that she shaves her head regularly to keep it silky smooth, but in reality all she does is wash her head and oil it to maintain the pristine bald look. What was immediately striking in the interview with Josanne

Figure 4.5 • Josanne Lochan

was that she was a very self-confident and self-assured young black woman who wore her baldness with pride and elegance. When asked if she ever considered wearing wigs to cover her baldness, Josanne replied:

> I would never dream of wearing a wig. At the end of the day you've got to feel comfortable in your own skin. It starts with you. If you're not comfortable with yourself, if you don't love yourself, then ultimately you're likely to have self-esteem issues. I must give credit to my mother who taught me and encouraged me to love myself; to see myself as beautiful as I am naturally. Thus if people don't like my image I don't take it to heart.

Once again, the interviewer was struck by Josanne's self-assured equanimity and the refreshing self-positivity she exuded in her answer to his initial question When asked whether she ever felt the pressure to conform, Josanne affirmed:

> I don't feel any pressure to conform, because I'm happy with the way I look. I think that I'm beautiful just the way I am, and ultimately that's what's most important. People either accept me the way that I am or they don't. Some people keep asking me, what on earth would possess you to ball off your head, but at the same time I get compliments from both men and women who say that I'm beautiful and that I'm pretty. So it just goes to show you that people have different perspectives on what is beautiful and what is not. What's important though as I've said before is that you

love yourself.

In answer to whether reactions to her baldness differed significantly depending on the country she was in, Josanne responded:

> Well, in the Caribbean region I seem to get the same general responses, but when I was staying in England it was real interesting. I would get a lot of people saying that I was exotic; that I had an exotic beauty. Now I found that to be nuanced, because on the surface while it might seem to be a compliment, it's not really a straightforward compliment. It's more like a backhanded compliment actually. It's basically saying that you're novel that you're out of the ordinary. So even though you being called beautiful, it's not your regular type of beauty, it's some sort of marginalized concept of beauty.

Chyna Whyne shared notably similar outward attributes, such as an unmistakable air of self-confidence and poise. She told the interviewer that in her case she had tried just about every hair style there was before settling on the bald look, and when asked point-blank what prompted her to shave her head bald in the first place, she replied:

> I had been through a lot of self-development, which included emotional and spiritual healing. I had built my self-confidence as a person and began to embrace my power as a woman and finally came to the realization that inner beauty was the key to my success. I use to place such emphasis on my external appearance, and my hair made me feel as though it determined who I was. The healing process that had taken place in my emotional state and my spiritual awareness prompted me to display the fact that my hair was not my beauty, and that my beauty was from within. After coming to this realization I went to a Jamaican barber shop in Croydon and asked them to shave my hair off. You can imagine the commotion. When my head was shaved, I took a look in the mirror and cried as it felt like this was the first time in my life that I recognized myself, with nothing to hide behind. It was almost as if I were naked.

This response prompted the interviewer to probe for a sense of the particular hair-styles that Chyna had tried before sporting the bald look. She replied:

> I had every hairstyle going, weaves, plaits, and various types of extensions, which leading up to me shaving my head, was beginning to concern me as I realized I was wearing other peoples dead hair on my crown. Energetically this had its own subtle disturbances, so far as I was concerned. Ever since that moment of

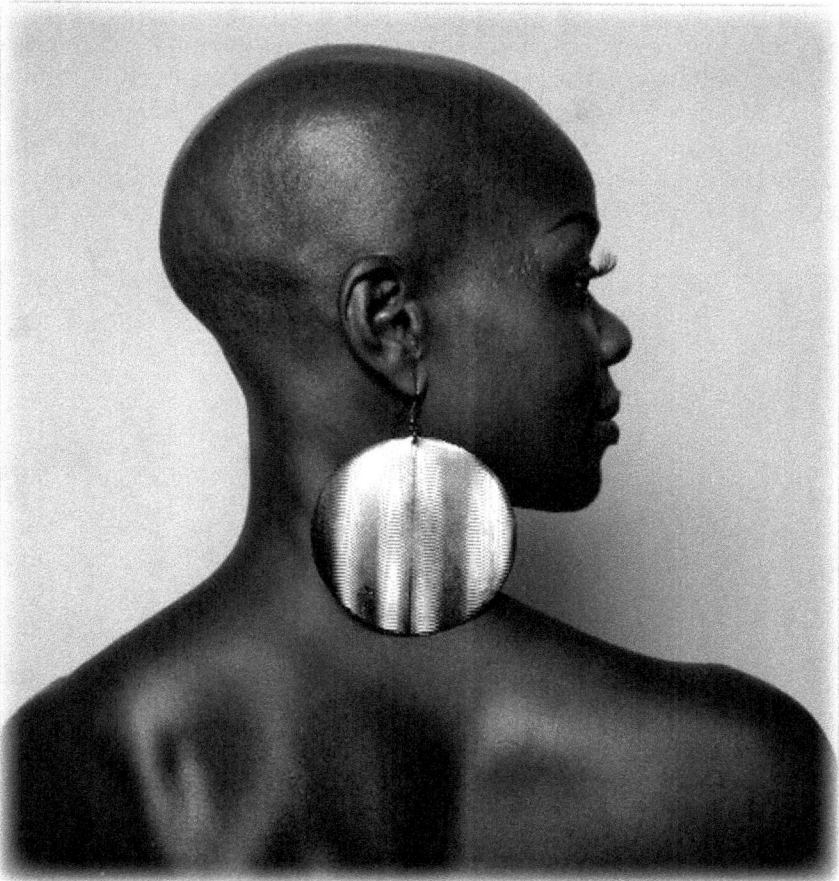

Figure 4.6 • Chyna Whyne

shaving my head bald (more than a decade ago now), I feel more liberated, feminine, beautiful, radiant and so confident sporting my bald head. Women and men continually compliment me on my bravery and beauty. Black women in particular are conditioned into believing that wearing false hair on their head is the way forward; however I do believe if one does enough spiritual and emotional healing, self-acceptance will prompt any woman to remove the false trappings that continues the diseased mentality that got us wearing weaves in the first place!!

Probably one of the most revealing conversations on hair that I had was with my research assistant, Kadine Ferguson. Out of all my respondents she was the only one that had transitioned from relaxed to natural and then back to relaxed hair in a relatively short couple of years. In other words, she had experienced wearing her hair both relaxed and in its natural state in relatively rapid succession. In my view she epitomized the complex product (or dialectic) of inner psychological forces and outer social forces that go to determine how black women wear and style their hair in Jamaican society. In a detailed testimonial, Kadine recounts her hair journey as follows:

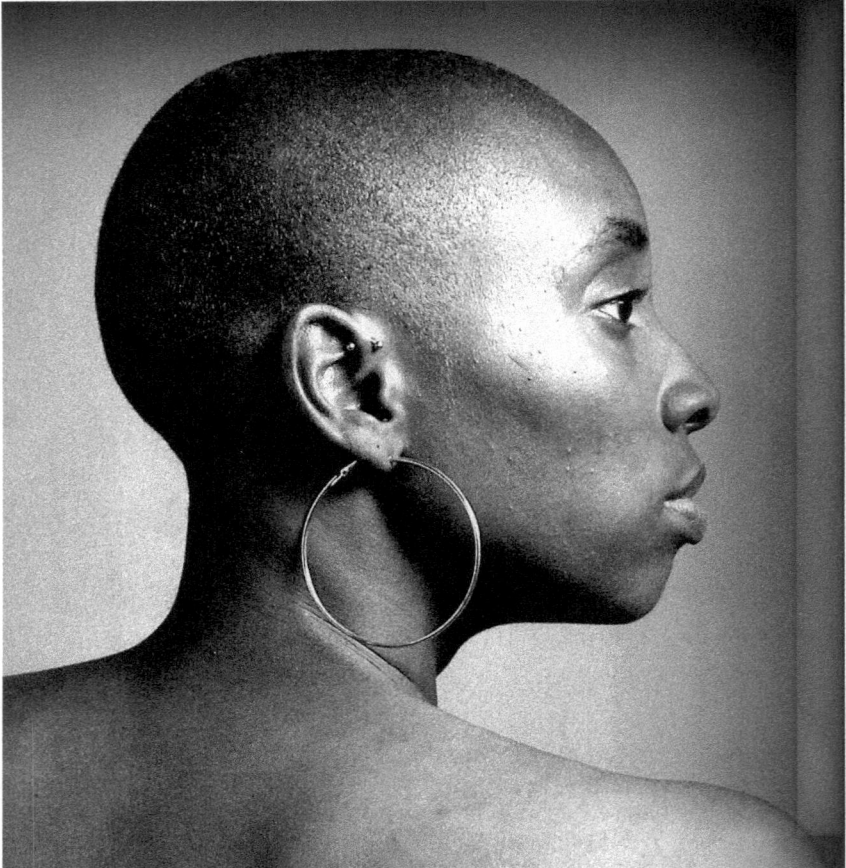

Figure 4.7 • Kadine Ferguson

For me, beauty is the ability to accept oneself as is. Of course, with the importance and emphasis society places on physical appearance, notably, complexion and hair texture, one cannot help but second-guess themselves. I have had and still have my own personal experience as it pertains to hair texture.

I was never a fan of chemically processed or texturized hair, but I did it back in grade 8 of high school, when I was 13. I was at that age where my family acknowledged that I was old enough to have such privilege. Please note, I equate getting one's hair chemically processed a privilege, because at age 13, it was the norm. All my peers got their hair texturized at that age. If your hair wasn't straight, long and 'bouncy' at age 13, you would've been teased by the other girls. I remember my hair being referred to as 'black-peppa grain' up until I got my hair chemically processed in high school. I remember feeling pressured. I also can recall feeling embarrassed by the texture of my hair and anyone can imagine my sense of relief when I was old enough to eliminate what seemed to be 'the root of the problem'.

I remember getting my hair chemically processed for the first time – yes, there was that sense of belonging or 'fitting in' as I knew I would no longer be faced with the mockery of having natural hair. I was frequently complimented on numerous occasions of how 'nice', 'long' and 'thick' my hair now looked. I agreed and thoroughly enjoyed all the compliments, but what overpowered that sense of 'belonging' was the fact that I could now act more independently in terms of styling my hair. To me, my hair became lighter, longer and more manageable and I no longer relied on anyone to comb my hair. I even rejected offers from my peers who expressed an interest to style my hair. It was almost as if styling my own hair and disallowing anyone in my hair was a form of retaliation against all the mockery I had previously faced.

I kept my hair chemically processed over the years and by the time I started my undergraduate studies, I felt totally liberated. Yet, I still had chemically processed hair for two and half out of the three years I was at the university. However, throughout the three years, the length of my hair got shorter. I was a student athlete and the maintenance of my hair was burdensome as I needed to treat my hair at least once per week. As my hair got shorter, my colleagues and family would always ask 'Why do you keep cutting your hair?' or 'You look better with long hair.' My response to my colleagues would always be a dry 'OK'. Or I'd usually tell members of my family that I want to 'wear my hair short' or 'I might go natural' – which would usually generate a response that indicated shock or disbelief.

It was in my last year of my studies at the university, it occurred to me that I wanted to have low natural hair. I had made observations of other students with natural hair on campus and I simply liked it. At the same time however, it seemed as if more and more female students were sporting the weave. Looking back, there seemed to be fewer students with natural hair but they stood out. What served as further motivation though, was the fact that people seemed quite opposed to me 'cutting off' my, what they would describe as a 'good body' of hair. I remember telling my friends that I was planning to go natural. One of them said, with a sense of humour, 'I won't walk or talk with you, if you do.' Another told me that I wasn't 'brave enough' to do it. The comments I received were generally like that. I wouldn't say these comments were negative but they were certainly discouraging; but as an 'individual' I didn't always require approval.

Finally, one early morning, sometime after 2am, I grabbed a scissors and cut off the remainder of my hair. At the time, I had what most people would've considered the 'Rihanna hair style' (very low sides and back with a fringe). I must have gone overboard because when I was finished, my hair was really low. When my friends first saw it, they were surprised because they didn't think I would've have done it. I was usually asked the question 'Why?' or 'Why did you cut your hair?' Months after, people kept telling me that I should 'grow back my hair' and they would then usually draw reference to the times when I had chemically processed hair. At one of my old jobs, a co-worker blatantly said I would 'look better with longer hair' and that my short hair portrays a certain image. I asked her to clarify what she meant by that and she said that my short hair made me look like a lesbian. For the most part though, I did receive some positive comments from the general public. Some men, with and without locks would even refer to me as 'empress'.

Having said that though, there was still a considerable degree of stigmatization and marginalization that I faced when I wore my hair short and natural, as opposed to when I wore my hair straightened and relaxed. For instance some female shop assistants seemed to go out of their way to shame me when I would enter the store, by continuously referring to me as 'Sir' when I think that it was perfectly obvious that they were talking to a woman. On other occasions I was treated as though I was invisible, not being given any due attention by the shop assistant, unless I made a concerted effort to assert my presence, by either talking more forcefully or adopting a 'no nonsense' persona.

Then there were all of these background comments that somehow you just weren't as feminine with your hair short, as opposed to when it is long and flowing. Comments expressing such sentiments came from both men and women and in some cases were not necessarily subtle.

Some members of my family (grandfather and grand-aunts)

were definitely not keen on my hair being short and natural, even though interestingly enough they were all devout church going Christians. 'So you ah turn Rasta,' was one of the remarks I received when I visited one of my relatives in the U.S. (my grandfather) in 2013. I soon got the message. Natural hair wasn't acceptable in his/their eyes, even if the hair was neatly combed.

When I finally got bored with my hair and decided to relax it again, it seems as though I was now more widely accepted, that I was able to fit in more with people's expectations. I am no longer regarded as some sort of rebel, but rather somebody who is more mainstream, somebody who can now fit into a wider variety of social circles. I am no longer the centre of attention all the time, or the object of snide remarks, rather I am just one of the rank and file in 'most any group that I immerse myself into.

In this regard I can say from first-hand experience that there still exists a not so talked about schism so far as wearing one's hair short and natural as a black woman in Jamaican society is concerned. To wear it 'natural' is the aberration, while to wear it 'relaxed' is the norm.

The final area that I would like to address, in so far as the matter of natural hair vs relaxed hair is concerned, turns the lens on Lupita Nyong'O.

THE LUPITA NYONG'O PHENOMENON

In 2014, after the highly acclaimed release of the cinematic portrayal of the slave narrative, *12 Years a Slave*, a young Kenyan actress by the name of Lupita Nyong'O shot to fame for her supporting role in the film, as the destitute slave, Patsey. After winning an Oscar for her role, Lupita's celebrity status was assured and she was notably heralded as a modern day beauty, gracing the front cover of women's magazines such as *Lucky, Dujour, Vogue, Glamour,* and very notably the front cover of *People*'s "50 most beautiful" issue (May 2014). She was also named the new face of Lancôme cosmetics in 2014 (to be more specific, she became the new ambassadress for the French cosmetic company, Lancôme, Paris).

These accomplishments are noteworthy and certainly worth mentioning as the reality is that Lupita represents a departure from the typical mainstream magazine front cover face of beauty. On the front cover of the *Glamour* December 2014 issue, one of Lupita's more profound interview remarks is quoted, viz., "There's room in this world for beauty to be diverse." And this is just what Lupita represents

– a type of beauty that is different from what can be regarded as the standard Euro-oriented beauty norms and ideals. First of all, she is dark-skinned; second, her hair is short and natural (that is, it is worn in its natural African kinky texture). There was a time not so long ago when the combination of these two factors alone would have almost certainly ruled her out as a front page model for mainstream women's magazines.

So why is Lupita all of a sudden being embraced by the mainstream media? Could it be a case of strategic tokenism in an attempt to appease some of the communities that lie outside the contours of whiteness? Or is it an effort to embrace beauty in all of its diversity?

Lisa Tomlinson in her article on Lupita's meteoric rise to stardom (*Huffington Post,* March 18, 2014) contends that she is skeptical of all the fanfare and fetishism that has accompanied the discourse concerning Lupita. She further argues, "As history has shown, mainstream media has systematically exoticized, racialized women for white consumption. I cannot help being suspicious that Lupita Nyong'o's beauty and accomplishments are being packaged as a token commodity."

In Leslie Bennetts' story "The Breakthrough: Lupita Nyong'o" featured by *Glamour* magazine in their December 2014 issue, the most telling part of the interview session, so far as this author is concerned, is captured in Lupita's response to Bennetts' question: "You've received lots of attention for your looks. Did you grow up feeling beautiful?" Her response was:

> European standards of beauty are something that plague the entire world – the idea that darker skin is not beautiful, that light skin is the key to success and love. Africa is no exception. When I was in second grade, one of my teachers said, 'Where are you going to find a husband? How are you going to find someone darker than you? I was mortified. I remember seeing a commercial where a woman goes for an interview and doesn't get the job. Then she puts cream on her face to lighten her skin and she gets the job! This is the message: that dark skin is unacceptable.

So what gave Lupita her sense of self-worth? According to her answer to this question in her interview with Julie Jordon and Antoinette Coulton for the 2014 *People* magazine special issue feature article, it was her mother. She says in the article (p.74): "My mother always said I was beautiful and I finally believed her at some point. She taught me that your presentation is an expression of how much you care about yourself and those around you."

Another source of inspiration for Lupita has been the African model, Alek Wek. During a speech at the *Essence* "Black Women in Hollywood" Luncheon, held in February 2014, Lupita credited the success of supermodel Alek Wek as a major boost for her own self-image. She said (*Vogue* magazine, July 2014, p. 90): "I remember a time when I too felt unbeautiful", and then went on to articulate the sensation of having a flower bloom inside of her when the Sudanese born model Alek Wek appeared on the modelling scene in the mid-nineties.

In her interview session for the special edition of *People* magazine's "World's Most Beautiful" issue, Lupita discloses that the compliments she remembers and cherishes the most are when she has been called beautiful with not one drop of make up on.

Lisa Tomlinson (2014) argues that through the mainstream media gaze, Lupita's moving story of the self-hate that she used to have for her dark skin has been re-branded as a 'Third World' dark skin girl narrative, essentially a 'feel-good' story, wherein a black girl from humble beginnings is able to overcome the adversity presented by hegemonic beauty ideals and gain some degree of self-worth. For Tomlinson (2014) this re-branding masks the complexity of the situation and the many layers of oppression that are actually involved. As such, not only are particularly pertinent strands of oppression obfuscated by this narrative, but almost inevitably the trivialization of actual structural forces of racial oppression and denigration at play also takes place.

For this author, while the Lupita Nyong'o phenomenon is a welcome development in terms of diversifying the depictions of beauty in the popular media, and promoting the notion that one can be beautiful with dark skin and African textured hair, it still amounts to tokenism. The odd dark-skinned model with African features, such as Alek Wek or Lupita Nyong'o, will not significantly stem the urge or tendency for black women to alter their hair texture (or even lighten their skin complexion) unless there is a plethora of Lupitas or Aleks in the media and in advertisements.

CONCLUSION

Importantly, Byrd and Tharps (2014) detail in an elaborate way just how culturally important hair was to both black male and female Africans prior to the onset of the trans-Atlantic slave trade. They observe (2014) how in the early fifteenth century, hair functioned as a carrier of important social and cultural messages in West African societies such as those of the Wolof, Mende, Mandingo and Yoruba.

Hairstyles essentially indicated things such as a person's marital status, age, ethnic identity, religion, wealth, and rank within particular communities or regions. The authors (2014) further note that in some communities a person's surname could be identified from their hairstyle as each clan would have their own unique hairstyle. Thus, when the Europeans started to visit the West African coast, they were impressed not only with the particularly diverse array of agricultural products that the Africans grew, but with the women's elaborate hairstyles as well. According to the French explorer Jean Barbot, the Senegal blacks "have their hair either curled or long and lank, and piled up on their heads in the shape of a pointed hat". He wrote further that the Qua-qua on the other hand "wore long locks of hair which they plaited and twisted and daubed with palm oil and red earth" (Byrd and Tharps, 2014).

The picture that is painted overall by Byrd and Tharps (2014) is that even when Europeans encountered Africans with next to no clothing, the hairstyles would almost always be extremely elaborate, intricate works of art, showcasing braids, plaits, ornate patterns shaved into the sides of the scalp, or even shells, flowers, beads as well as strips of material woven into the hair.

Of interest is that with the onset of the trans-Atlantic slave trade, where millions of Africans were forcibly removed from the West Coast of Africa (from Senegal down to Angola), many of the captured Africans (both men and women) had their heads shaved against their will by the European slave traders or by African captors who were complicit in the slave trade. Given the importance of hair to Africans, having their heads shaved would be tantamount to a most heinous and unspeakable crime, and it does not take any stretching of the imagination to know that such an act would not only be an indignity, but also emotionally traumatic. This act was a deliberate part of the process of stripping the captured Africans of their identities and making them more compliant and easy to control. According to Byrd and Tharps (2014 : 10), shaving the heads of their newly captured slaves was the first step that the Europeans took to erase their culture and identity and bring about a sense of self-alienation. By separating the slaves from family and community, from their homelands in Africa, and then from themselves by forcibly shaving off their intricate hairstyles, total alienation was ensured. After enduring the horrors of the Middle Passage, suffering the indignity of being completely naked and shorn of their signature hairstyles, Mandingos, Fulanis, Ibos and Ashantis would enter the new world, just as the Europeans intended, like anonymous chattel.

In my opinion, many of us Africans in the Diaspora who are the descendants of slaves have never really recovered from the initial trauma that our ancestors first experienced when they were enslaved and forcibly stripped of their identities and sense of self. Many of us are still suffering from self-alienation or what DeGruy (2005) refers to as the post-traumatic slavery syndrome. On top of this, we have been taught to be ashamed of anything that is indigenously African, whether it be the clothes, the hairstyles or even the religions (that still exist in repressed syncretic forms, in many cases masked as more widely accepted religions such as Catholicism). As such, even though natural African textured hairstyles are growing in popularity, they still are not as widely accepted or as widely regarded as the permed or processed (creamed) and weave-based hairstyle common in largely black communities or societies.

I believe that black people will not be able to move away from the insidious "good hair/bad hair" dichotomy unless they are able to embrace their own natural hair and other physical features collectively. In order to do this they will need to overcome centuries of accumulated self-alienation, be prepared and if necessary bold enough to carve out their own symbols, their own models, and their own ideals of beauty.

Notes

1   See *Jamaica Observer* (2013).

2   Black History Month Forum 2012, "Notions of Beauty in Black Communities Globally: Rituals of Positive Affirmation and Denigration of the Black Body", held Friday, February 24 at the Mona Campus of the University of the West Indies.

3   Black History Month Forum 2013, "Hair Stories: Exploring Pervasive Attitudes Towards Hair and Beauty Within Black Communities", was held Friday, February 22 at the Mona Campus of the University of the West Indies.

References

Abdullah, A. S. 1998. Mammy-ism: A diagnosis of psychological mis-orientation for women of African descent. *Journal of Black Psychology* 24(2):196-210.

Banks, Ingrid. 2000. *Hair Matters: Beauty, Power and Black Women's Consciousness*. NY: New York University Press.

Bryd, Ayana, and Lori Tharps. [2001] 2014. *Hair Story: Untangling the Roots of Black Hair in America*. New York: St Martin's Press.

DeGruy Leary, J. 2005. *Post Traumatic Slave Syndrome: America's Legacy of*

Enduing Injury and Healing. Milwaukee, OR: Uptone Press.

Erasmus, Z. 1997. Oe! My hare gaan huistoe: Hair styling as black cultural practice. *Agenda* 32:11-16.

Fanon, Frantz. 2008. *Black Skin, White Masks*. London: Pluto Press

Miller, Errol. 1969. Body image, physical beauty and colour among Jamaican adolescents. *Social and Economic Studies* 15(1):72-89.

Nehusi. K. 2002. Mental enslavement. In *Emancipation*, ed. David Granger. Georgetown, Guyana.

Rooks, Noliwe. 1996. *Hair Raising: Beauty Culture and African American Women*. NJ: Rutgers University Press.

Tafari-Ama, Imani. 2006. *Blood Bullets and Bodies: Sexual Politics Below Jamaica's Poverty Line*. Kingston, Ja: Multimedia Communications.

Tafari-Ama, Imani. 2016. Historical sociology of beauty practices: Internalized racism, skin bleaching and hair straightening. *IDEAZ* 14:1-19 (this vol.).

Tate, Shirley-Ann. 2009. *Black Beauty: Aesthetics, Stylization and Politics*. Surrey: Ashgate Publishers.

Thompson, C. 2009. Black women, beauty, and hair as a matter of being. *Women's Studies* 38(8):831-856.

The Internet

Donaldson, Chanel. 2012. Hair alteration practices amongst black women and the assumption of self-hatred. NYU, SteinHardt, Applied Psychology Programme: OPUS. Accessed May 3, 2015 (http://steinhardt.nyu.edu/appsych/opus/issues/2012/fall/hairalteration).

Grenee, H. Fields. 2011. What spending a half a trillion dollars on hair care and weaves says about us. *Madame Noire*, 11 May (http://madamenoire.com/57134/what-spending-a-half-a-tril-lion-dollars-on-hair-care-and-weaves-says-about-us/)

Newspapers and Periodicals

Glamour (magazine). 2014. Lupita: The breakthrough (December):234-239.

Henry, Davina. 2013. Not so sexy, naturally: Unprocessed hair not perceived as sensuous for female entertainers. *The Gleaner* (16 June).

Jamaica Observer. 2013. Jamaica weave imports set to hit $I billion in 2013. Business Section (1 November).

People (magazine). 2014. 50 most beautiful people. 81(18, May 5).

Silvera, Janet. 2012. Police women fight to wear Afrocentric hairdos. *The Gleaner* (26 February).

Vogue (U.S. edition). 2014. Grace notes (July):86-99.

Cinema

Rock, C., Kevin O'Donnell, Jeff Stilson, Lance Crouther, Chuck Sklar, Cliff-Charles, Marcus Miller, Roadside Attractions (Firm), HBO Films, Zahrlo-Productions, Urban Romances (Firm), Lions Gate Entertainment (Firm), et al. 2009. *Good Hair* [Motion Picture]. Santa Monica, Calif.: Lions Gate Entertainment.

CROSSING BORDERS, BLURRING BOUNDARIES

Comparative Meanings of Beauty in Brazil, South Africa and Jamaica

DOREEN GORDON

Abstract   This article considers comparative meanings of beauty among upwardly mobile black people in Brazil, South Africa and Jamaica. Visual aspects of status negotiation are significant in all three contexts, where the African body has long been represented at the bottom of racial and cultural hierarchies as ugly, closer to nature, oversexed, and animalistic – in direct opposition to the supposed aesthetic dominance of the European body. This has meant that upward mobility often translates into downplaying African physical features as much as possible. However, various social and political movements in these countries have contributed to an expansion of possibilities for black upward mobility and expression of identity. Given their potentially strategic position, do contemporary black elites challenge racialized hierarchies through their beauty practices? In what ways do their beauty practices stress or erase differences? The main argument of this article is that consumption around beauty is one way in which emerging black elites assert their belonging as equal citizens, as well as establish links with the world.

Key words • Oversexed • Black body • Identity
           • Beauty practices

IDEAZ Vol. 14 • 2016 • ISSN 0799-1401 (101–132)
© Centre for Tourism & Policy Research / Ian Boxill – UWI, Mona

INTRODUCTION

My interest in the topic of physical appearance and beauty stems from a concern with the significance of visual aspects of status negotiation in highly racialized societies – how is race and class "read" off of bodies, and how might persons deploy physical appearance and self-styling as they negotiate racialized hierarchies? In order to examine these issues, the article explores the links between ideas about beauty, "race", and class in three different postcolonial locations: Brazil, South Africa and Jamaica. In each of these contexts, social constructions of race shape social inequality, though in different ways. I attempt to show how the different racial formations found in Brazil, South Africa and Jamaica produce specific ideas about race and beauty. At the same time, a comparative approach reveals the ways in which these meanings emerge from similar conditions and experiences across the black Atlantic.

This article is part of a larger research project that focused on the conditions and circumstances surrounding the emergence of contemporary black elites in Brazil, South Africa, and more recently, Jamaica. This project examined strategies of social mobility and identity formation among persons self-identifying as black middle class, utilizing an ethnographic approach focused on the collection of genealogies and family histories, participant observation in both personal and public social spaces, semi-formal interviews, and informal conversations. An unexpected finding arising from the analysis of data in all three contexts was that beauty and physical appearance – especially as it relates to dress, skin colour, hair, and body/physical features – emerged as a meaningful category in people's everyday lives – especially for black women living and working in spaces associated with whiteness and upper class privilege. In the social stratum in which I moved, practices and discourses of beauty were particularly significant and underscored deeper, politicized issues about "race", visibility, social mobility and citizenship. Drawing selectively on literature about the birth of mass consumption in Europe and America (Benjamin. 2006; Heinz, 1990; Strasser et al., 1998; Zelizer, 1997), I put forward the general hypothesis of this paper: that consumption around beauty is one way in which emerging black elites (coming from previously marginalized social positions) assert their belonging as equal citizens as well as establish links with the world.

This article therefore gives attention to the multiple meanings of beauty across class positions. Given their potentially strategic position, do upwardly mobile black people challenge racialized hierarchies through their beauty practices? Or do beauty practices emphasize old as well as newer inequalities? For example, some observers suggest that powerful racial legacies and the internalization of white supremacist classifications have influenced the recent growth of a lucrative hair and skin bleaching industry among black people across the Diaspora (Banks, 2000; Charles, 2003, 2009; Erasmus, 1997). Indeed, discourses about "race" have long been associated with ideas of beauty and physical appearance. The black body in particular has frequently been represented as "ugly", closer to nature, oversexed, and animalistic – in direct opposition to the supposed aesthetic dominance of the European body (Nuttall, 2006; Hobson, 2005). Certain physical features associated with "African" heritage have been negatively valorized – such as having tightly curled, kinky hair and a broader nose. This has contributed to an ongoing stigma and a sense of low self-esteem among black populations (Charles, 2003; Hall, 1995).

In addition to the racialization of certain physical features, other aspects of appearance have been integral to the construction of social difference and status in colonial and postcolonial contexts – such as dress, ways of styling the body, etiquette, and ways of speaking (Buckridge, 2004; Fanon, 1967; Ribane, 2006). Although important in other contexts around the world, these practices take on special significance for the negotiation of status in black Atlantic societies. The following example taken from Nelson Mandela's autobiography, *Long Walk to Freedom* (1995), underscores the importance of physical appearance for poor black South Africans subjected to extreme forms of racial discrimination, exploitation and exclusion in apartheid South Africa.

In his autobiography, Nelson Mandela (1995) recalls the day he successfully completed his first degree at the University of South Africa in 1943. The first thing he did was to buy a new suit. For many years he could not afford it, even though he was working as a clerk in a Jewish law firm in Johannesburg. A lawyer handed him an old suit to help with his working wardrobe – a suit that he wore almost every day for five years and which ended up having "more patches than suit" (Mandela, 1995: 90). So ashamed was he about the state of his clothing that he wrote about how he tried to avoid an old classmate of his as he was walking home from work one day:

> I was embarrassed by my threadbare clothing and crossed to the other side, hoping she would not recognize me. But I heard her call out, 'Nelson... Nelson!' I stopped and crossed over, pretending that I had not noticed her until that moment. She was pleased to see me, but I could tell that she observed how shabby I looked (Mandela, 1995: 90).

Mandela again wore the symbolic Western suit when he was released from prison after 27 years, indicating his change in status. On the other hand, dress could also be used as a powerful symbol of resistance. During the Rivonia trial, when Nelson Mandela and other prominent members of the African National Congress

(ANC) were being tried for treason, terrorism and sabotage, his wife's appearance in court attracted as much attention as the legal proceedings. It was reported in the *Post* (5 April 1964) that Winnie Mandela turned up in court dressed in traditional Xhosa attire, thus emphasizing African pride. The judge, realizing the impact of this powerful visual imagery, banned her from wearing such clothes to court (Ribane, 2006: 48). As Mandela assumed the leadership of the ANC after his release from prison, he became known for the colourful silk shirts he wore, dubbed the "Madiba shirt". It was a clear repudiation of Western style clothing. This story underscores the point that people are not just the victims of racial ideologies, discrimination and oppression. Indeed, "race" as a principle tends to force people into boxes, obscuring the complexity in practice. Detailed ethnographic research can give insight into the varied ways that people negotiate everyday inequality in their societies.

Feminist theories have long contributed to approaches to beauty within the social sciences. Only a few publications (for example, Taussig, 2012) have begun to explore how men are impacted by and participate in discourses and practices of beauty. For many theorists, beauty's meaning in women's lives continues to be a problem. On the one hand, feminists have argued that beauty ideals and practices reflect patriarchal domination (Bordo, 1993; Wolf, 1991). These analyses stress slightly different arguments but seem to coalesce on the point that beauty practices act as a means of social control over the female body. On the other hand, beauty is also seen as a potentially pleasurable instrument of female agency (Cahill, 2003; Gimlin, 2002). These writers emphasize women's subjective experiences of beauty and how they might derive personal satisfaction from body work. This view of beauty as a tool of agency has proved illuminating for my work. Beauty practices and discourses represent an important means through which respondents could have a constructive impact on their everyday experiences, defining a space for individual action and for circumventing traditional inequalities. More recently, feminist writing has been focusing on the "pragmatics" of beauty – that is, "how is beauty defined, deployed, defended, subordinated, marketed or manipulated" (Colebrook, 2006: 132). This has been a particularly useful approach in writing this article. What people do on a daily basis throws light on how they create, cope with and resist racial discrimination in their own countries – as well as how they establish connections with the world. This article contributes to a growing body of scholarship focused on theoretical and empirically grounded comparative work, contributing to an understanding of race and racism in a more global sense.

THE COMPARATIVE LENS

Although clearly not the same, the history of black populations in Brazil, South Africa and Jamaica are interrelated. For example, "race" has structured patterns of inequality in all three countries. The author recognizes that different historical and social processes, as well as colonial histories shape these nations; indeed, cultural constructions of "race" are not directly transferable across national borders. At the same time, comparative research provides opportunities for asking questions about common experiences and global hierarchies of power that perhaps could not be articulated otherwise. In particular, Africans and the African diaspora have tended to be ranked at the bottom of global hierarchies of races, ethnicities, cultures and nations. Broadly speaking, this hierarchy is based on an international ranking according to political, economic, and cultural prestige and power (Basch, Glick Schiller and Szanton-Blanc, 1994). This global racial-cultural hierarchy places Anglo-American culture at the apex and Sub-Saharan African culture at the base. Other cultures (usually with their own complex and dynamic internal hierarchies) jostle to occupy intermediate positions between the two extremes (Brodkin, 1999; Frankenberg, 1997). Global discourses about race and culture clearly affect the contours of local hierarchies in the countries discussed in this paper – even as what happens in countries of the Global South potentially challenges the hegemony of Western capitalistic centres (for example, emerging non-white elites on the global scene in recent decades).[1]

Greater disposable income among middle income earners in emerging economies such as Brazil and South Africa has created a favourable environment for growth in the beauty and personal care industry. Unilever, an Anglo-Dutch multinational beauty company, generates more than half of its sales in emerging and developing markets, with a large presence in Brazil, India, South Africa, Argentina, and Turkey (Reuters, January 21, 2014).[2] Brazil ranks high when it comes to a preoccupation with the body, beauty and physical appearance. In 2007 Brazilians spent US$22 billion on hygiene and cosmetic products, making the country the third largest consumer of cosmetic products in the world. In the same year, more than 700 thousand persons underwent some kind of plastic surgery in that country (Machado-Borges, 2009: 211). Meanwhile, the market for beauty and personal care in the Middle East and Africa has expanded, with international brands such as L'Oréal, Estée Lauder and Revlon increasing their stakes in major cities (Reuters, July 31, 2013). Estée Lauder, for example, has launched top luxury brands such as Clinique and MAC in major African cities such as Lagos. The managing director of Estée Lauder for Sub-Saharan Africa told Reuters in an interview that there is "a massive interest from consumers in international brands [and] our target consumer is the emerging middle class, the established middle class and that affluent African consumer who's probably well travelled and very brand savvy" (Reuters, July 31, 2013).[3] According to UNISA's Bureau of Economic Research in South Africa, South Africans' personal care spending in 2000 was ZAR$13.5 billion, which included the black hair industry (*City Press, May 9, 2004*).

Jamaica has been severely impacted by economic recession in recent decades, even though World Bank reports register a 50% jump in the number of people joining the middle classes in Latin America and the Caribbean.[4] Jamaica's economy has been characterized by slow growth and high debt over the last two decades.[5] However, this state of economic affairs has not hampered spending on beauty, underscoring the significance of this aspect of social life in Jamaica. According to recent trade statistics, the island officially imported US$7 million worth of wigs and hair weaves in 2012, up from US$3.3 million in 2008. The importation of this product is up to fourteen times higher than other Caribbean countries and exceeds annual car imports from South Korea into the island (*The Jamaica Observer*, Friday November 1, 2013).

I will now outline for the reader the methodology and research context from which my ethnographic examples will be drawn. I have carried out work on emerging black elites in Salvador, Brazil (2005-2007); in South Africa in the cities of Pretoria, Johannesburg and Durban (2011-2012); and more recently in Kingston, Jamaica (2013). These are quite different cities with their own local dynamics that required a flexible approach to studying "race" and "class". I adopted similar strategies: I lived in and visited different neighbourhoods and interviewed persons across racial categories, age, gender and social background. This allowed greater insight into residents' cognitive maps of their cities and how they grounded their sense of being middle class. I also participated as much as I could in the lives of a small sample of families whose members self-identified as black middle class. I met the individuals and families involved in my research through my initial contacts, moving along their kinship and friendship networks in order to meet other respondents. I gathered 40 family histories and genealogies in Brazil and 25 in South Africa. In addition, I participated in their lives as much as possible, attending family gatherings, dinners, weddings, baptisms, art galleries, restaurants, bars, and churches. In South Africa I gave special emphasis to social interaction in public spaces such as malls, neighbourhood functions, restaurants, public transportation and private parties, as under apartheid there were restrictions on movement. It was therefore important to observe racially mixed post-apartheid urban spaces. Finally, local television shows, lifestyle magazines and newspapers were invaluable sources of information.

In Brazil and Jamaica, the legacies of slavery and conquest have created similar racial formations (Beckford, 1972; Wagley, 1957). Brazil enslaved more Africans than any other American nation and was one of the last countries to abolish slavery (in 1888).[6] Despite the significant contributions of African descendants to economic, cultural and social life, they have long been marginalized, to varying degrees, from national processes and equal citizenship. With limited opportunities for upward mobility in colonial settings, strategies of "whitening" became a means by which African descendants could improve their lives and social position. This could be achieved through physical whitening – for example, by marriage to lighter skinned spouses, thereby producing lighter skinned offspring; or symbolic whitening, through adopting the lifestyles and values of the elite and acquiring wealth and education. Either way, such persons could cross racial boundaries to some extent by their association with whiteness. It has been argued that it was easier for light skinned persons to move up the ladder than darker skinned persons – a theory that has been called the "mulatto escape hatch" (Degler, 1971).

The existence of upwardly mobile non-white individuals in the higher social classes has been used as a key plank in arguments for racial democracy in Brazil (Wade, 1997). Yet Africans were widely denigrated, seen as "forever constituting one of the causes of our inferiority as a people."[7] Anxious to be counted among modern and progressive nations, official Brazilian state policy encouraged European immigration in an effort to "whiten" the population. When Brazil's population remained far from white, elites cultivated an image of the country (especially between the years 1900 and

1950) as the world's first racial democracy (Andrews, 2004; Telles 2004).

Salvador occupies a particular position within this Brazilian racial formation. It is associated with a strong black identity and culture, due to its history as a major slave and commercial port. While Salvador appears more favourable than most places in Brazil towards African descendants, social inequalities have long been described as extreme and entrenched (McCallum, 2005). The majority of the population are both poor and visibly darker skinned, while economic power resides in the hands of a Euro-Brazilian elite (Figueiredo, 2003). Therefore, blackness can be experienced as ambiguous – as both empowering and oppressive. Although Brazil collects data on race in the national census, Brazilians tend to classify themselves into a range of flexible groupings along a spectrum of colour and other phenotypic attributions (Harris, 1970; Sanjek, 1971).[8] This has given rise to over 150 terms used informally to distinguish between different skin shades – such as *cor de mel* (colour of honey) *cor de canela* (colour of cinnamon) and *café com leite* (coffee with milk). Black movement activists state that this is due to Brazilians' desire to distance themselves from blackness. However, this is tempered in a city like Salvador where many of the younger generation identify with blackness (Sansone, 2003).

Caribbean societies are largely composed of transplanted peoples from Africa, Asia and Europe, so that political and intellectual elites did not have a long tradition from which to draw upon in terms of constructing national identities. A "creole" culture developed in which Eurocentric values, including the superiority of whiteness, were emphasized. On the eve of Jamaica's independence from Britain, social stratification in Jamaica continued to reflect this legacy. Errol Miller's classic study in the 1950s of Jamaican adolescents' concepts of beauty and body image illustrates that regardless of ethnic background, they had all assimilated to a creolized ideal of beauty that emphasized a European appearance.[9] Furthermore, satisfaction with their body image was based on its closeness to a light skin complexion (Miller, 2001). This discourse continues today, although there have been broad socio-political changes, including ideological challenges to the colonial racial order by the black and Rastafarian movements during the 1960s and 1970s. The rise of a black political, professional and entrepreneurial class in recent decades has also complicated the picture (Gordon, 1987; Robotham, 2010).

Jamaica today represents a country in which persons of African descent are in the majority and control state power. Since the mid-twentieth century, opportunities have steadily opened up for Afro-Jamaicans such that a national black bourgeoisie is taking its place. Nevertheless, colonial and postcolonial orders in the Caribbean established a colour-class hierarchy in which hegemony was legitimized in terms of the superiority of things European, the inferiority of Africa and African-derived traditions. Jamaica established a white, brown and black hierarchy based on the colour of one's skin. This had meant that the brown segment enjoyed certain privileges under slavery which carried over into post-slavery society. By the 1990s, however, black elites increasingly emerged on the political scene – yet economic wealth remained in the hands of brown and white elites. In this sense it might be compared to South Africa, where emerging black national elites have political power, but the economy is still in the hands of whites (Robotham, 2010). In this postcolonial environment where "race" and "class" identities are dynamic and unstable, physical appearance becomes a significant way of expressing belonging and citizenship in the nation.

Unlike Brazil and the Caribbean, South Africa has had minimal experience with slavery except in the Cape. Competition and conflict between colonial powers in South Africa led to less stability than existed in Brazil where the consistent maintenance of Portuguese rule helped to reduce internal conflict (Marx, 1998: 45). Brazil's colonial legacy of greater unity and state centralization brought greater stability to race relations than was the case in South Africa. In fact, some analysts of Brazil, such as Freyre (1986a; 1986b), have claimed that the Portuguese were more modest in their racial prejudice than the British, resulting in lower levels of racial strife. However, contemporary literature on race relations in Brazil has challenged this claim, emphasizing the widespread existence of racial discrimination and inequality (Hasenbalg and do Valle Silva, 1999; Telles, 2004). Nevertheless, this has not been imposed legally – at least in the twentieth century – unlike South Africa or the segregationist American South. This is not a trivial distinction – when racial discrimination is mandated by law, it operates in a more rigid and inflexible way than in societies in which it is informal and at the discretion of individuals. At the same time, the informality of racial discrimination has made racism difficult to name in Brazil. In this instance, beauty practices might provide a viable strategy of negotiating racialized hierarchies, especially in a society where racism is often denied or unclear.

What is distinctive about the racial formation in South Africa was the institutional effort put into maintaining white privilege while holding down the wages and living standards of the African majority (Feinstein, 2005). Under both colonialism and apartheid, living space was allocated on racial grounds, with each group of non-whites being assigned their own areas and Africans in particular being confined to townships with inferior service provision. For decades, formal categories of race were used to classify South Africans (Black African, White, Coloured, and Indian/Asian). The South African apartheid government used race to classify people by law into a general hierarchy of types with correspondingly differential access to human rights and freedoms. While those classified as white were full citizens and those classified as coloured and Indian were partial citizens, "Africans", who were at the bottom of this structure, were considered for the most part tribal subjects.

Apartheid discourse made race real materially by entrenching unequal access to housing, employment, remuneration, education, health and other social services. However, lived reality sometimes defied apartheid's pure types. People resorted to using the system of racial classification to pass for white or coloured in order to access the rights and opportunities associated with these legal categories (Erasmus, 2008). Racial categories largely correlated with class. For example, the black workforce was largely restricted to unskilled and low-paid employment in agriculture, mining, and services. Indians and coloureds filled an intermediary sector of employment. When South Africa emerged from apartheid, the Black Economic Empowerment programme was instituted in 1996 as an affirmative action policy that sought to increase the numbers of non-whites in the public and private sectors. Formerly white residential areas were opened up and public spaces in general became more racially mixed than before. The race and class basis of social inequality has therefore been changing slowly. A black middle class has emerged, building on older origins.

Today, Brazil and South Africa are emerging economies that are adding a new dynamic to the global capitalist order. Yet both countries are highly unequal. In Brazil, modern social and economic indicators continue to demonstrate significant disparities between blacks and whites despite recent economic growth (Reichmann, 1999). In South Africa, blacks have emerged out of extreme forms of racial segregation and discrimination under apartheid. The black middle class belongs to the national majority, yet there is much debate about the nature of this state-made elite – sometimes referred to as "black diamonds", a term reflecting the lavish lifestyle and high-end consumerism of the politically empowered elite. Some – such as Mbeki (2009) – claim that this elite is more alienated than ever from the masses of poor, black people. Indeed, the black elite is often critiqued in the media for its opulence, vulgarity and lack of style. For example, the annual opening of parliament in Cape Town is a post-apartheid phenomenon. Before South Africa became democratic 20 years ago, the opening of parliament was a conservative and heavily militaristic affair. Since 1994 the event has become increasingly colourful, with a high fashion component evolving over the years, showing pride and excitement in the new parliament. However, the local newspapers cover the event with disparaging remarks about some of the fashion choices. The *Sowetan Live* (February 11, 2011) stated: "The opening of Parliament is Cape Town's annual fashion show, where politicians don their best or sometimes display their lack of fashion sense." Last year, a journalist for the *City Press* (February 18, 2013) wrote that Zuma's wife, Thobeka Madiba, was dressed in a "boob-bearing peach dress" which was "too everything – tight and revealing". He rated her fashion choice as the "Most inappropriate First Lady Outfit".

Physical appearance and self-styling is therefore hyper-emphasized for the black elite in South Africa. Their situation recalls historical accounts of the birth of mass culture in the United States and Europe in the late nineteenth and early twentieth century, when the middle and working classes had to be taught how to consume (Strausser et al., 1998; Zelizer, 1997). This literature emphasizes the role of advertising and brands in forming consumer behaviour – a phenomenon that is ever present in South Africa today. Malls, department stores, the media, lifestyle magazines, financial institutions, the automotive, telecommunications and beauty industries, international companies and brands now target a section of the population who were formerly excluded from certain urban spaces and consumption of particular goods under apartheid.

In a study of Jewish immigration from Eastern Europe to New York in the twentieth century, Heinz (1990) shows how participation in American mass consumption was one way for this community to express attachment to the new society. The abundance of commodities was – and probably still is – a marker of North American identity. This could be particularly relevant for black people seeking to affirm their new social positioning in post-apartheid South Africa. They link themselves to the nation and to the rest of the world through the consumption of a wide array of local and international brands. In the following section, I will now take the reader into the ethnography of the article, illustrating how my respondents negotiated everyday inequalities.

KEEPING UP APPEARANCES

On a breezy afternoon in November 2006, I stood in the foyer of the Teatro Castro Alves, a historically important theatre located in the north eastern city of Salvador in Brazil. The theatre-goers chatted while drinking cups of coffee. The women in particular were dressed in their finest evening wear, with slim bodies and salon-straightened hair. When members of the Teixeira family walked into the foyer, they represented some of the fewer darker-skinned faces in the crowd but they did not look out of place. Indeed, they were described by their friends as a particularly stylish, sophisticated and educated family. On this afternoon, they were dressed elegantly, makeup carefully applied, a hint of perfume, smart handbags, high-heeled shoes and expensive sunglasses perched on top of their well coiffed hair. In a country obsessed with svelte and sensual bodies, they blended easily into the crowd, exuding confidence, style and glamour. Eventually, Juliana, the matriarch of the family, introduced me to a tall man standing beside her, "This is Alberto, the plastic surgeon who totally reformed my breasts and stomach after my divorce. His hands are like magic, he is a great artist. I am very happy with my results." Alberto smiled and lifted his cup of coffee to hers.

While plastic surgery is subsidized by the public health system in Brazil, those who can afford it go to private clinics where the cost could vary from US$6,000 upwards (Machado-Borges, 2008: 152). In speaking openly about her plastic surgery, Juliana was presumably making the point that she was financially able to participate in the consumption of this particular beauty practice in a country where plastic surgeons have been known to state that "everyone has a right to beauty" (Edmonds, 2007, 2010). Indeed, one of the more distinctive things about the Teixeiras was the manner in which they presented themselves and managed their bodies – their dress, physical appearance, body language and speech. Juliana stated that she never left her house without her hair being well groomed (meaning, chemically straightened and dyed black), her skin looking good, and her clothes fashionable. I was first introduced to Juliana's three daughters, all in their thirties, at the party of a Brazilian friend who explained: "They are different from the common person here in Salvador. You can tell because they are *bem educado*. Look at how beautiful they are!"[10]

According to Juliana, the Teixeira family is descended from an original union between an African slave woman and the son of a wealthy Dutch sugar plantation owner. This man subsequently married a white woman but all of the children from the former union were well taken care of. Juliana's parents lived a comfortable life and were respected in their neighbourhood – her father was university educated, worked for a British shipping company and spoke many languages, while her mother was an educator. They maintained a relatively privileged position for generations. Juliana acknowledged that they have had to downscale in the current economic environment. But none have become poor. Indeed it could be said that they have reformulated their status over time. By selective consumption of particular items of cultural value and by social networking, the Teixeiras manage to negotiate their status in the middle classes.

Juliana stated that in the past, family members preferred to refer to themselves as *mulato(a) claro(a)* (light skinned/mixed race). She remembered that as a child, she sometimes heard relatives make disparaging remarks about the physical features and moral traits of darker-skinned persons. These racialized discourses surrounding appearance and the valuation of particular, physical traits possibly indicate strategies among non-white elites to distance themselves as much as possible from the negative valuation of blackness and racial discrimination, although they did not always escape it. For example, Juliana related that many years ago her mother, Rita (who had since passed away), tried to gain entrance into one of Salvador's most exclusive social clubs, located in an upscale area of the city. Rita had many long-standing, influential friends among the Euro-Brazilian elite who were members of the club. One of them was the *prefeito* (mayor) of Salvador and he wrote a letter recommending Rita as a member. Nevertheless, the executive committee of the club rejected Rita's application. Her friends were indignant and were convinced that their friend's skin colour was the deciding factor. To protest the club's decision, they immediately withdrew their membership.

This story related by Juliana is potentially revealing of everyday social relations in many ways. First, it indicated how personal relationships across lines of colour and class (such as friendships, kin ties) could sometimes mitigate the negative effects of having darker skin colour, though it did not always protect them from feeling discriminated against. Second, it could be the case that Rita's friends did not perceive or treat her as black – in other words, she had become structurally and symbolically "white" by virtue of being seen as a member of their class. Therefore, the story indicates that there were instances in which persons could cross racial boundaries as they become upwardly mobile.

Some generations later, the growth of an increasingly vocal black movement as well as the adoption of legislation against racism and policies directed at reducing racial inequality have led to a more positive valuation of blackness in Brazil (Sansone, 2003; Telles, 2004). The younger generation of the Teixeira family claims a more politicized, black identity – symbolized by their use of the Brazilian Portuguese term *negro* – while challenging others in their family to take on this identity. For example, they criticized their mother's brother, Bruno, for describing himself as *Brasileiro* (Brazilian), which is a way of stating his claim to a mixed race identity, in line with dominant national discourses prevalent amongst his generation. Younger people, however, would be more familiar with an international, multicultural discourse of "race", especially since the UN Declaration of Human Rights in 1948 and the subsequent introduction of multicultural policies into the constitutions of many Latin American nations (Kymlicka, 1995).

Unlike her brother, Juliana identified as *negra* and indicated that racial prejudice persists, illustrating her point by referring to the discriminatory way that lighter skinned shop owners treat her when she enters their expensive stores to shop. Yet, she emphasized the family's indigenous heritage when explaining the frequent comments made by others about their "good looks". She made reference to the high cheek-bones, petite frame and "finer" hair that many women in the Teixeira family possessed, associated with an Indigenous rather than an African background. Here, a statement is being made about culturally preferred physical features, in which the lowest rank is assigned to an appearance associated with an African heritage – such as tightly curled, kinky hair. Darker-skinned persons might therefore distance themselves from unflattering associations with blackness, claiming an indigenous heritage instead.

It was not uncommon for contradictory discourses about

"race" to exist within the same context – an identification with blackness and a distancing from the more stigmatizing meanings of blackness. What is interesting about the case study above are the different ways in which persons negotiated unequal society in Salvador, employing discourses or practices centred on the body to erase or stress difference. In this sense, persons could move across racial boundaries or categories depending on the context. However, it was a lot more challenging for my respondents in South Africa to transcend racial boundaries, as I will illustrate below.

As the summer was drawing to an end in May 2012, I was invited to a pool barbeque in Pretoria – a typical middle class South African affair where I met Hope, an attractive, middle aged woman with a lively and warm personality. Eventually I told her about my interest in studying the black middle classes in South Africa, and she declared that she would be my first interviewee. She invited me to one of her famous dinner parties at her upscale home in the northern suburbs of Johannesburg, and we subsequently met several times. Originally from the city of Durban on the Pacific coast of South Africa, she described her family as having mixed ancestry – East Indian, White and Zulu. They were classified as coloured by the South African government, and this required them to live in a coloured township with other mixed race people. She described her mother as a housewife, coming from a well-to-do family with substantial land as well as cattle, poultry, livestock and horses. Her father's family was less wealthy. He worked as a middle level administrator in a local company. However, despite their comfortable standard of living, they were marginalized under South Africa's apartheid regime and had to negotiate the limited amenities, services and opportunities available to them as coloured South Africans. Negative stereotypes about coloured people abounded – such as their supposed propensity for alcohol, violence and promiscuity. However, Hope's mother was determined to give her a good life. Her mother always had an excellent command of English and she made sure to pass on this skill to Hope, as many persons from the township could not speak or write in English. Reflecting on her life, Hope felt that this ability to speak English had been beneficial in her professional and personal life, allowing for some mobility. She applied to work as a receptionist in a travel agency during the 1980s. This propelled her into the social world of White South Africans, since they were principally the ones who could afford to travel. She recalled that, at first, her clients were often surprised at seeing who she was after speaking to her on the phone. They did not expect to see a coloured woman in that setting, carrying herself confidently and possessing the required language skills to move in their context. In this working environment, she was required to attend social gatherings, speak well and dress elegantly. She wore her hair long and blow dried it straight, and shopped in city boutiques. She spent 10 years in this environment which was enough time to get to know some of her clients – indeed, some invited her to their parties and she began to make friendships. However, she had to delicately navigate the racial divides in such social settings. For example, she told me that her friends would often say to her, "We don't see you like we see them [black South Africans]", expecting that Hope would also share this view. While she had access to these social settings, in apartheid South Africa you had to return to the neighbourhood to which you were designated, according to your racial classification. One evening, a senior manager offered to take Hope home in his car. They were stopped by police and taken to the police station under the suspicion of being an interracial couple. One of the policemen described Hope as being a "Transkei beauty queen".[11] At the time, interracial sexual affairs were illegal under the Immorality Act. When it became clear that they were just friends, the police let them go. Racial boundaries were therefore difficult to cross in a legal system of racial segregation. It is not surprising therefore that even as Hope increasingly socialized among privileged, white social circles, her first marriage was to a black South African.

Eventually, Hope went into television broadcasting as a news reporter. She was chosen for this position because of her ability to speak English and because she presented a pleasing visual appearance, as she was told by one of her managers. However, her visual appearance did not suit the media industry when apartheid came to an end in 1994. They were looking for a different image, one that promoted black pride and black African culture, one that would reflect South Africa's new society. Her ability to speak English was not necessarily seen as an asset as indigenous African languages began to be celebrated. She had to find other job opportunities, mostly working in sales and advertising. Her first marriage ended, and she moved to Johannesburg to pursue other opportunities, eventually meeting and marrying a Portuguese entrepreneur and moving to London to live with him. The couple had a daughter, Maya, and lived in London for 6 years. However, this second marriage did not last, and Hope returned to South Africa, this time to set up her own business as a human resources consultant. She found abundant opportunities for work, sensitizing the staff of major companies to diversity in the post-apartheid workplace. She currently coaches business executives and managers – especially black entrepreneurs who now have access to new economic opportunities through the Black Economic Empowerment programmes of the South African government. In the competitive business world of Johannesburg where executive boardrooms are still primarily white and male, she assists black South Africans who want to learn how to negotiate these environments successfully and confidently. She focuses on their physical appearance (dress, skin tone, hair, and personal grooming) as well as speech, body language and etiquette. Indeed, Hope's physical appearance is one of the main ways in which she markets herself – she makes sure that her skin, hair and nails are always maintained in good condition and that her clothes are fashionable because she must present to her clients a convincing and successful image of herself. Hope mentioned a case where she had to advise a black executive woman to get her teeth straightened and whitened, as an essential component of her image in the business world. In the case of another business client who attended high profile social events, Hope gave advice on fashion labels and cosmetics. These stories reflect the anxieties of a post-apartheid society where changes in status and the visibility of previously marginalized groups of people in the city led to a hyper-emphasis on appearance.

Hope is the manager of her own business and is in high demand. Defining herself as a black woman, she has been able to take advantage of government policies that are specially geared towards black women (black women have been targeted for special programmes due to double discrimination). Hope argues that anyone who was not white under apartheid is black, because all non-whites were formerly subjected to racism and repressive policies. She has built a successful and comfortable life for herself, living in formerly privileged White neighbourhoods and able to take vacations at her beach home in Port Elizabeth, a popular seaside town in the Eastern Cape province – a far cry from her life growing up in a depressed Coloured township in Durban. Her daughter Maya, on the other hand, has grown up in a more privileged environment, attending private schools and circulating in social contexts where many of her peers are white or light skinned. Hope worries that Maya does not see how she is different to others in her social circle, and that one day she could come face to face with some serious racism which she would be ill-equipped to deal with. When I asked Maya, who at the time was 13 years old, what she thought of her mother's racial identification as black, she scoffed and wrinkled her nose – it was clear she did not think much of this idea. Maya described herself as mixed race, an identification which could be influenced by her experience in Europe and the fact that her father is Portuguese. To counteract Maya's upbringing in a largely White upper middle class environment, Hope has several works of art as well as musical collections by black South African artists and bookshelves throughout the house stacked with literature on South Africa's diverse history, culture and peoples – especially the struggles of black South Africans for freedom.

To summarize from the above case studies, it is clear that Hope had less opportunity in her society to cross racial barriers or categories in comparison to my respondents in Brazil who never experienced situations such as separate residential areas and enforced segregation. However, there are some ways in which their experiences are similar. Hope's social mobility, as well as that of the Teixeiras, is connected to their links to white culture and society. After the end of the apartheid regime, Hope could change her racial identity from coloured to black South African. Similarly, my Brazilian respondents were also reflecting on and challenging their own racial identifications in a changing environment that allowed for a more positive valuation of blackness. Finally, both cases illustrate that physical appearance can be deployed as a kind of social capital as respondents attempted to negotiate highly unequal societies – even though at times physical appearance could be the basis of discrimination.

THE "AESTHETICS" OF RACE

A discourse on the "aesthetics" of race is common to Brazil, South Africa, and Jamaica. This refers to the ways in which different body parts are valued – that is, the shape, colour, and size of different physical features – which has long been central to ideas about social difference, status and self-worth in postcolonial contexts. Physical features associated with blackness have been negatively valued within this schema. This is believed to contribute to beauty practices such as skin bleaching or lightening. Despite the documented physical, medical and psychological effects of this practice on the body, it continues to be a problem in many countries across the African diaspora (Charles, 2003, 2009; Glenn, 2008; Ribane, 2006). Skin bleaching is dealt with extensively by other authors and will not be discussed in this article (see also Hall, 1994, 1995; Mire, 2001).

The link between ideas about beauty and constructions of "race" has had a long history. Nineteenth century theories about race emanating from Europe juxtaposed European civilization with African savagery and barbarism. These ideologies had various strands, but converged on the idea of European superiority and beauty (Jarrín, 2010; Wade, 1997). Therefore, the first register in which discourses of beauty need to be understood has to do with the inscription of Africa in dominant Western aesthetic discourses as the figure of the ugly. In his 1764 essay, "On National Characteristics So Far As They Depend Upon the Distinct Feeling of the Beautiful and the Sublime", Kant argues that different "nations" have different aesthetic and moral sensibilities. The "beautiful" and the "sublime" are for him qualities of aesthetic and moral "feeling", both of which, he concludes, Africans lack. The African, he writes, "has no feeling beyond the trifling", which he links to "the ugliness of appearance" in the time of European colonization and beyond (Nuttall, 2006: 9). The African continent is therefore portrayed as the metaphor par excellence for ugliness and moral decay. According to these accounts, ugliness and decay were particularly visible in the black body. Nowhere is this more emphasized than in the case of the "Hottentot Venus" – the famed South African Sara (or Saartjie) Baartman, a Khoisan woman who was brought to England and France for public exhibition between 1810 and 1815 (Gilman, 1985). The "Hottentot Venus" came to symbolize both the presumed ugliness and heightened sexuality of the African race. Baartman's body was exhibited in nineteenth century freak shows to display her large buttocks and her "African" physical features, seen to be the opposite of femininity and beauty in Europe (Hobson, 2005: 1).[12]

The second register in which beauty discourses need to be understood is that Western theories of the beautiful came to be mediated through the figure of blackness. For example, Simon Gikandi has argued that when Pablo Picasso, master of European modernism, began to draw inspiration from African art in a movement later known as primitivism, it was the terror – and the disgust – African objects made him feel that inspired him (Nuttall, 2006: 9). The psychoanalyst Franz Fanon (1967), writing about racial being in the aftermath of European colonialism in Africa, mentioned the "white look" that renders the black person a source of terror and desire. Indeed, European fears of racial degeneration and regression into black primitivism were expressed in theories of scientific racism. For example, Arthur de Gobineau (1816–1882), who spent fifteen months in Brazil as France's envoy, commented that, "We are dealing with a totally mulatto population, corrupt of flesh, and frightfully ugly" (Schwarcz, 1993: 5). The Jamaican contribution to this kind of discourse can be found in the writings of Edward Long (1734–1813) and Bryan Edwards (1743–1800), both of whom wrote histories of the island. Obsessed with racial purity, Edward Long was highly critical of whites mixing with other races. To him, the unnatural mixture of the races has produced, in Spanish America, a "vicious, brutal, and degenerate breed of mongrels" (Beckles and Shepherd, 2000: 551).

At the same time, the eroticization of the black and mixed raced woman was part of these discourses. For example, the rise of African American performer, Josephine Baker, in the years between World War 1 and World War 11 emphasizes this contradictory discourse. Josephine Baker came to popularity during an era of heightened interest in American jazz, Brazilian music, the Harlem renaissance, black sexuality and African dance as symbols of an avant-garde culture in Paris. Although this mixing of cultures was celebrated on Parisian stages, its duplicity should not be underestimated – the exotic was preserved as such, an adoration combined with domination (Hobson, 2006; Nuttall, 2006). Josephine Baker's body threatened Europe's civilization, and her nudity and wild dancing elicited outrage in such cities as Berlin, Vienna and Prague, where she was denounced as the "black devil". In her dancing, she recreated popular stereotypes of the black female savage, but also mocked the West's obsession with black female bodies, poking fun at white hegemonic discourses of beauty.

In commercial ports and major sites of colonization, the mixed race woman or *mulata* (as she was referred to in Brazil) became part of the grammar of the exotic. However, in these contexts, race and beauty were drawn together in a hierarchy of appearance which firmly put black bodies at the bottom. A folk taxonomy of colour terms developed in Brazil in which fine distinctions are made between skin colour and physical features, often indicating the status and worth of the person. Terms that refer to darker skin colour have traditionally been negatively valued. However, in Brazil, as well as in many Latin American and Caribbean countries, racial markers such as skin colour, hair, and facial features are not necessarily conclusive. Economic success and other forms of upward mobility can "whiten" dark-skinned persons in ways that did not obtain in other countries such as the United States or South Africa.[13] Therefore, Brazilian racial classificatory practices are often described as fluid, descriptive and situational in comparison to notions of race grounded in ancestry entailed within the "one drop" rule in the United States, or the enforced legal segregation of an apartheid regime in South Africa.

The *morena* (mixed race woman) is the quintessential icon of a long-standing ideology of racial democracy in Brazil, portrayed in eroticized in images of carnival, samba, and football both in Brazilian popular culture and in the global media.[14] The meteoric rise of Brazilian celebrity Andressa Soares in recent years, whose stage name is Mulher Melancia (Watermelon Woman), epitomizes this national obsession with the mixed-race woman. A dancer, singer and model known for her unique style of dance, Mulher Melancia seems to possess the desirable traits of the *morena*: tanned skin; long, flowing hair; large, rounded bottom; and ability to dance in an erotic manner. This presents an alternative scenario for feminist theory. While studies on the relationship between "race" and beauty exist (Banet-Weiser, 1999; Banks, 2000), feminist writers have tended to emphasize the dominance of Euro-American beauty standards that reinforce the desirability of fair skin, small noses and lips, and long hair. While this discourse is not absent in Brazil, a cultural logic of "race" exists that celebrates mixture and eroticises brownness. The *morena* supposedly combines all the positive characteristics of each race in Brazil. In this construction of national identity, some aspects of blackness are valorized. For example, a cousin of the Teixeira family, whose fair complexion and blonde hair allows her to make a claim for whiteness, proudly tells people that "*Eu tenho a bunda do negro*" (I have the bottom of a black person).

In Jamaica, heightened efforts of nation building during the 1960s among artists and political and intellectual elites focused on creating a national creole identity, as in the national motto, "Out of many, one people". Beauty pageants were symbolic constructs of the nation. In a pageant organized by the *Daily Gleaner* in 1955 entitled "Ten Types, One People", ten contestants were selected that the organizers felt reflected the island's range of racial and colour diversity. For example, "Miss Ebony" was described as "a Jamaican girl of black complexion"; "Miss Mahogany, a Jamaican girl of cocoa-brown complexion"; "Miss Golden Apple, a Jamaican girl of peaches and cream complexion"; "Miss Apple Blossom, a Jamaican girl of white European parentage"; and "Miss Lotus, a

Jamaican girl of pure Chinese parentage" (quoted in Barnes, 2006: 64-65). Yet beauty pageants have continued to yield consistent criticism for selecting beauty queens that represent Eurocentric beauty values. However, a cultural preference for a voluptuous body with a well rounded bottom (or "batty" in Jamaican parlance) is well noted and taken rather seriously in Jamaican discourses of beauty and desire. Although a rising fitness and gym culture focusing on slimmer bodies is taking place especially in urban areas, popular culture continues to celebrate the "fluffy" woman, such as in the 2014 carnival calypso song by DJ Killa, "I Want a Rolly Polly". The song's lyrics glorify a generous and curvy female shape:

Ah want ah fat gyal,	*I want a fat girl,*
Ah want ah Rolly Polly,	*I want a Rolly Polly,*
Ah want a big gyal,	*I want a big girl,*
you make me bawl holy	*you make me shout holy*
molly.	*molly.*

Whether in working class dancehall settings or more middle class carnival celebrations, female bottoms are let loose in uninhibited, glorious celebrations of flesh and sexual energy. Even though such displays have historically been characterized as riotous and disorderly, such movements of the "batty" in the contexts of dancehall and carnival invite a public discourse that challenges colonial constructs of decency and white supremacy.[15] The very essence of black women's dancing threatened systems of class, gender, race, and nationality. Less feminine and disorderly dances were relegated to the margins – looked down upon by black, mixed-race and East Indian elites alike who imagined a more feminine public persona that supported efforts towards national identity. Beauty competitions emerging in the decades before colonial independence emphasized feminine and decorous roles. Brown or mixed-race women asserted a more respectable presence that countered the disruptive black body.

The social value of whiteness coexists with national discourses of race mixture in Brazil and Jamaica, and is related to historically important strategies of social mobility. For example, one of my respondents in Salvador, Maria, was adopted into a modest, land-owning family. Her first marriage was to a man she described as *branco* (white), with whom she had a daughter. Today she is remarried to a man she described as *negro* (black). However, in informal family gatherings, she rarely referred to her sons resulting from the second marriage. Maria talked mostly about her daughter

– who is lighter-skinned with blonde hair. She indicated that her daughter was beautiful and would *fazer sucesso* (make a success of herself). Here she makes a link between her daughter's socially acceptable physical appearance and her potentially successful mobility in the future, underscoring the gendered character of upward mobility.

These old colour hierarchies reappear in the contemporary, highly competitive work market in Salvador, in the hyper-emphasis on *boa aparência* (good appearance). Traditionally, *boa aparência* meant having lighter skin combined with certain signs of a higher social class position. This concept has particular meanings for female employees in the modern service and financial sectors that have blossomed to cater to Salvador's up and coming middle class (Edmonds, 2010; Telles, 2004). Employees have to reflect an image of modernity, cosmopolitanism and glamour associated with city centre lifestyles. Varying in shade from dark brown to light, shop assistants, cashiers and salespersons are mostly slim, smooth skinned and young with straight or long hair.

Similarly, whiteness or an association with European physical features garners value in Jamaica. For example, two studies (Cramer and Anderson, 2003; Gopaul-McNicol, 1993) have shown a preference for lighter skin tones in Jamaican children who were asked to identify their preference for a black and white doll. Cramer and Anderson's study (2003) is interesting for the breakdown across age, rural/urban background and gender it provides. They found that there was favouritism for white skin in older rural children (mean age 11.4 years) compared to younger rural children (mean age 5.6 years) – perhaps indicating learned values associating whiteness with beauty and goodness occurring as children get older. However, the older children in the urban area (mean age 10.9 years) showed a preference for black skin. The urban kindergarten children equally selected the black and white dolls when they were asked about their ideal self. The rural fifth and sixth grade children showed favouritism for white dolls. This difference between rural and urban settings might indicate a more conservative racial formation in rural Jamaican parishes. Rural and urban boys (as compared with girls) saw the white targets as "nice". Here, a preference for lighter skin colour is notable among the boys. Indeed, Mohammed (2000) has argued that light skin complexion is still important in male-female relationships. Mulatto women in Jamaica (the product of miscegenation between blacks and whites during the colonial period) are now the "browning" in contemporary culture. These brown-skinned women are still the objects of desire for many black men.

HAIR

Across participants in all three countries, hair texture was regarded as one of the most important, visible signs of the social aesthetic power of a woman and is related to meaningful symbols of femininity. Long, wavy or salon straightened hair is generally preferred, especially in the urban areas where it is associated with modernity and glamour. For example, the popular South African soap opera, *Generations*, is a melodrama about the power struggles of two wealthy black families in Johannesburg. Urban ideals of femininity are reflected in the show's most central characters – such as Dineo, a single woman constantly searching for a boyfriend (and ultimately a husband). She is very beautiful, well dressed and glamorous, the editor of a fashion magazine. Her hair is mostly worn straight or wavy – long or short – always in a style associated with sophisticated lifestyles. My respondents often achieved this appearance by sewing or gluing hair extensions from China, Brazil and India unto their natural hair. In a discussion about hair and intimate relationships among my South African friends one evening, they noted that the men they were involved with preferred this look as the relationship became more serious.

Meanwhile, tightly curled, kinky hair – is frequently associated with an African heritage and defined as socially ugly and unfeminine. In Brazil, the terms *cabelo ruim* (bad hair) and *cabelo duro* (hard hair) are used in reference to curly textured hair. Indeed, it was not long ago when, in July 1996, an album released in Brazil included a song, "Veja os cabelos dela", by Tiririca, a Brazilian singer, comedian and politician. While popularly regarded as playful and humorous, the song included a number of negative stereotypes about black women, highlighting the gendered dimensions of racism. The song refers to a woman who initially captures the singer's attention, but whose hair he finds undesirable, likening it to a scouring pad used to clean pots and pans. His description of her also makes reference to her smell and skin colour, such as:

Essa nega fede,	*This black woman stinks, she*
fede de lascar,	*stinks horribly,*
Bicha federenta,	*Stinking beast,*
fede mais que gamba.	*she smells worse than a skunk*

The song associates black bodies with ugliness and stench,

and in particular, stigmatizes the texture of black women's hair. The lyrics created an outcry amongst black activists and resulted in both Tiririca and his recording label, Sony Music, being sued for racism. However, the song was not seen as offensive by most Brazilians, but rather as a *brincadeira* (joke). Indeed, Brazilian discourses of "race" have frequently used humour in order to transmit racist stereotypes (Goldstein, 1999; Sheriff, 2001).

The idea of at least "taming" the black characteristics of the body took on added significance for the upwardly mobile. Straightening the hair – through hairstyling, the application of chemicals, or use of wigs and long hair extensions – was one such beauty practice that could modify appearance. The link between straight hair and a kind of raced and classed femininity (closely associated with a "European" appearance) was enacted by participants' beauty practices but not explicitly stated.

However, multicultural discourses of race that promote blackness as a source of pride have led to some changes. For example, Brazilian black feminists have organized workshops on hair-braiding and natural hairstyling, underscoring efforts to challenge dominant prejudices regarding the hair texture of black women (Caldwell, 2007). These efforts have had varying effects. The popularity of blonde hair extensions among women who are the target of these efforts underscores the need to evaluate more closely conditions of power in the lives of lower versus middle class women.

Nevertheless, the increased promotion of beauty practices that express pride in blackness has challenged hegemonic models present in Brazilian society that have tended to highlight lighter skin colour and hair. An expanding black beauty industry (occurring in Brazil and elsewhere) seems to have arisen to address this need (Dos Santos, 2000; Gomes, 2006). The contemporary concept of *beleza black* (black beauty) – which derives from African American civil rights struggles during the 1960s – is associated with these black movement discourses. It also reflects links between the black movement in Brazil and a more broad-based pan-African movement (Sansone, 2003). Cultural organizations in the city emphasize blackness as a source of pride and beauty as their members march through the streets in African-style fashion featuring bold prints and colours, their hair in braids and decorated with bright beads. The idea of un-straightened hair has gained currency among some participants, especially with the increased availability of hair care products now on the market. Hairstyles such as the afro, braids and dreadlocks signify the embrace of an alternative ideological code of value. Some professional women – like educators, doctors and lawyers – wore their hair in this way. However, it should be noted that women in a more powerful, socio-economic position perhaps have more options to challenge the racial status quo than women in low income communities whose options for social mobility are more constrained.

Moral arguments have been put forward that those with straightened hair want to cultivate a "European" appearance and are therefore suffering from low self-esteem and a mutilated black consciousness. Yet respondents asserted their right to style themselves in whatever way they felt like without being judged for it. For example, Nyla – a Jamaican respondent – grew up in a rural community on the western end of the island. Her mother came from a humble background in a sugar cane district and her father came from a comfortable family of farmers. As she got older, her mother decided to take her to the capital city of Kingston where she could access more opportunities. They lived at first with an aunt in a poor neighbourhood in Western Kingston while her mother tried to negotiate Nyla's access to higher quality education. Nyla did well and passed her examinations for an elite secondary high school in Kingston. In this environment, she was acutely aware of her dark skin and the neighbourhood she lived in. For example, she remembered that while she was a teenager, she went out on a date with a young man from one of Kingston's highly ranked boy's schools. When it was time to drop her home, she noted his growing scorn as he entered her neighbourhood. Nevertheless, her mother's marriage to an older man provided some protection and family stability for Nyla. She did well in high school, eventually enrolling in the Law Faculty at the University of the West Indies. When she graduated from Law School, she met her husband. His story is similar to Nyla's, in that he has achieved considerable professional success against great economic odds. Her marriage cemented their arrival at a higher social position – but this also entailed some anxieties about appearance. She was concerned about maintaining a slim body type and suitable image as a professional woman and wife of an influential man. She experimented with various hairstyles, including blonde and red highlights, coloured contact lenses, and fashionable clothes with international labels like Calvin Klein and Gucci, in line with her new status. Nyla currently uses Brazilian hair extensions for achieving her desired appearance, prompting one of her friends to comment that she was becoming addicted to "hair crack". However, she stressed her desire to experiment with different styles and fashions, stating that she has a right to choose how she wants to look.

From a post-feminist perspective, these participants might be seen to be adopting depoliticized stances towards social inequalities in their country. In *The Aftermath of Feminism*, Angela McRobbie (2009) argues that consumer culture in contemporary society offers the illusion of "freedom of choice" when in reality new forms of power are enacted that re-establish patriarchal hegemony and the cultural dominance of whiteness. However, elements of creative play involved in participants' beauty work are neglected in this perspective. Applying blonde highlights or implanting long hair weaves are also ways of inverting dominant beauty standards. In other words, some participants resisted their positioning by others to a certain racial category or appearance.

CONCLUSION

In this paper, I attempted a comparison of beauty practices and discourses in Brazil, South Africa and Jamaica. While recognizing that cultural constructions of "race" and of blackness differ across time and context, a comparative lens allows us to pose questions about similarities and differences across the black Diaspora that might otherwise not be articulated. The article revealed how my respondents crossed or blurred racial boundaries through their beauty discourses and practices. Beauty practices could also be used to stress or erase difference depending on the social context. The ethnographic material shows that this seemed easier for Brazilians and Jamaicans than for South Africans where black people experienced enforced segregation. Black middle class people both appear to challenge as well as accept racial inequalities in their society.

The close relationship between articulations of nationhood, gender and ideas about beauty are significant. Thus, national ideologies are both racialized and gendered in particular ways. The contradictory position of black middle class women – as representing both a marginalized and an economically better off stratum of the population – poses some complex issues for interpretation. Notions of femininity in particular are tied to traditional ideas that privilege a "European" appearance. However, recent shifts in racial thinking have made it less problematic to identify with blackness. Alternative notions of beauty emanating from the West – such as the African-American concept of "black beauty" – have mixed with local discourses to produce a more positive valorization of blackness. Some respondents embraced these discourses, while others resisted being classified as belonging to any particular racial category when it came to their beauty practices. They asserted the right to choose from a variety of options, which is suggestive of the need to further examine the impact of rising consumer culture and neoliberalism on local subjectivities. Writers who analyse the contemporary dynamics of post-feminism such as McRobbie (2009) suggest that consumer culture appeals to ideas about female success and choice while it in fact reinforces traditional power dynamics and ties women into new, neurotic tendencies (such as eating disorders). In the case of research participants, consumption focused on the body (beauty treatments, fashion, surgery) represents symbolic and material ways of positioning themselves within their societies as well as relating to the world – thus becoming "visible" like any other citizen.

Notes

1. A new World Bank report (2012) stated that Latin America and the Caribbean registered a 50% jump in the number of people joining the middle classes in the last decade. More specifically, the middle classes in the region grew to an estimated 152 million in 2009, compared to 103 million in 2003. See the following link: http://www.worldbank.org/en/news/press-release/2012/11/13/new-world-bank-report-finds-fifty-percent-increase-middle-class-latin-america-over-last-decade

   Meanwhile, the African Development Bank estimates that Africa's middle classes, numbering 115 million in 1980, has grown to 326 million in the past three and a half decades. Despite this rapid growth, Africa still has the smallest middle classes as a share of the total population. According to the African Development Bank, the African middle classes account for 33% of the population of the region, while in Asia this figure is 56% and in Latin America, 77%. See the following link: http://www.ft.com/cms/s/0/49812cde-c566-11e3-89a9-00144feabdc0.html#axzz39XH88G61

2. http://uk.reuters.com/article/2014/01/21/uk-unilever-results-idUKBREA0K09A20140121

3. http://uk.reuters.com/article/2013/07/31/esteelauder-africa-idUSL6N0G15E120130731

4. http://www.worldbank.org/en/news/press-release/2012/11/13/new-world-bank-report-finds-fifty-percent-increase-middle-class-latin-america-over-last-decade

5. http://www.worldbank.org/en/country/jamaica/overview

6. Over the course of slavery's existence, nine to twelve times as many Africans were imported into Brazil as into the United States. See Andrews (2004: 6).

7. Nina Rodrigues, *Os Africanos no Brasil* (1977).

8. The "race"/colour categories used in the Brazilian national census are *branco* (White); *pardo* (Mixed Race/Brown); *preto* (Black); *amarello* (Asian/ Yellow); and *indigena* (Indigenous).

9. Errol Miller used the following racial categories in his study: White, Brown, Black, Chinese and Indian.

10. This Brazilian Portuguese term refers to having both formal education and a sense of etiquette and cultural knowledge.

11. Transkei was a Bantustan or homeland set aside for members of a specific ethnicity in the southeastern region of South Africa, created as part an apartheid policy of "separate development". In 1994, it was reintegrated into its larger neighbour, Eastern Cape province.

12. More recently, Baartman became a national symbol when her remains were repatriated to her country of origin and laid to rest in 2002.

13. In the United States, having one drop of "black blood" in your family identified you as black, regardless of skin shade. In South Africa, racial categories were enforced by segregation and policies of racial discrimination such as the hair comb test, making it difficult to cross from one racial category to another.

14. For example, African American singers Snoop Dogg and Pharrell Williams promoted Brazilian mixed race beauty in their music video, *Beautiful,* set in Rio de Janeiro.

15. The term "batty" has recently taken on a more negative meaning, however, especially in homophobic expressions that describe gay men as "batty boy".

References

Andrews, R. 2004. *Afro-Latin America, 1800-2000*. New York: Oxford University Press, Inc.

Banet-Weiser, S. 1999. *The Most Beautiful Girl in the World: Beauty Pageants and National Identity*. Berkeley: University of California Press.

Banks, I. 2000. *Hair Matters: Beauty, Power and Black Women's Consciousness*. New York and London: New York University Press.

Barnes, N. 2006. *Cultural Conundrums: Gender, Race, Nation and the Making of Caribbean Cultural Politics*. MI: University of Michigan Press.

Basch, L., N. Glick-Schiller, and C. Szanton-Blanc. 1994. *Nations Unbound: Transnational Projects, Postcolonial Predicaments and Deterritorialized Nation-States*. Anghorne, PA: Gordon and Breach.

Beckford, G. 1972. *Persistent Poverty: Underdevelopment in Plantation Economies of the Third World*. London: Oxford University Press.

Benjamin, W. 2006. *The Writer on Modern Life: Essays on Charles Baudelaire*. Cambridge MA: Harvard University Press.

Bordo, S. 1993. *Unbearable Weight: Feminism, Western Culture and the Body*. Berkeley: University of California Press.

Brodkin, K. 1999. *How Jews Became White Folks and What That Says about Race in America*. Piscataway: Rutgers University Press.

Buckridge, S.O. 2004. *The Language of Dress: Resistance and Accommodation in Jamaica, 1760-1890*. Jamaica: University of the West Indies Press.

Cahill, A.J. 2003. Feminist pleasure and feminist beautification. *Hypatia* 18:42-64.

Caldwell, K.L. 2007. *Negras in Brazil: Re-envisioning Black Women, Citizenship, and the Politics of Identity*. New Brunswick: Rutgers University Press.

Charles, C. 2003. Skin bleaching, self-hate, and black identity in Jamaica. *Journal of Black Studies* 33:711-728.

Charles, C. 2009. Skin bleachers' representations of skin colour in Jamaica. *Journal of Black Studies* 40:153-170.

Colebrook, C. 2006. Introduction: Special issue on beauty and feminist theory. *Feminist Theory* 7:132-142.

Cramer, P., and G. Anderson. 2003. Ethnic/racial attitudes and self-identification of black Jamaican and white New England children. *Journal of Cross-Cultural Psychology* 34:395-416.

Degler, C. 1971. *Neither Black nor White: Slavery and Race Relations in Brazil and the United States*. New York: Macmillan.

dos Santos, J.T. 2000. O negro no espelho: imagens e discursos nos salões de beleza étnicos. *Estudos afro-asiáticos* 38:49-65.

Edmonds, A. 2007. The poor have the right to be beautiful: Cosmetic surgery in neoliberal Brazil. *Journal of the Royal Anthropological Institute* 13:363-381.

Edmonds, A. 2010. *Pretty Modern: Beauty, Sex, and Plastic Surgery in Brazil*. Durham and London: Duke University Press.

Erasmus, Z. 1997. Oe! My hare gaan huistoe: Hair styling as black cultural practice. *Agenda* 32:11-16.

Erasmus, Z. 2008. Race. In *New South African Keywords*, ed. N. Shepherd and S. Robbins, 169-181. Johannesburg: Jacana Press.

Fanon, F. 1967. *Black Skin, White Masks*. New York: Grove Press.

Feinstein, C.H. 2005. *An Economic History of South Africa: Conquest, Discrimination and Development*. New York: Cambridge University Press.

Figueiredo, A. 2003. A classe média negra não vai ao paraíso: trajetórias, perfis e negritude entre os empresários negros. Doctoral thesis, IUPERJ/UCAM, Rio de Janeiro.

Frankenburg, R. 1997. *Displacing Whiteness: Essays in Social Change and Cultural Criticism*. Durham, NC: Duke University Press.

Freyre, G. 1986a. *The Masters and the Slaves*. Berkeley: University of California Press.

Freyre, G. 1986b. *The Mansions and the Shanties*. Berkeley: University of California Press.

Gilman, S. 1985. *Difference and Pathology: Stereotypes of Sexuality, Race and Madness*. Ithaca: Cornell University Press.

Gimlin, D. 2002. *Body Work: Beauty and Self-Image in American Culture*. Berkeley: University of California Press.

Glenn, E.N. 2008. Yearning for lightness: Transnational circuits in the marketing and consumption of skin lighteners. *Gender and Society* 22:281-302.

Goldstein, D. 'Interracial' sex and racial democracy in Brazil: Twin concepts? *American Anthropologist* 101:563-578.

Gomes, N. L. 2006. *Sem perder a raiz: corpo e cabelo como simbolos da identidade negra*. Belo Horizonte: Auténtica.

Gopaul-McNicol, S. 1995. A cross-cultural examination of racial identity and racial preference for pre-school children in the West Indies. *Journal of Cross-Cultural Psychology* 26:141-152.

Gordon, D. 1987. *Class, Status and Social Mobility in Jamaica.* UWI, Mona: Institute for Social and Economic Research.

Hall, R.E. 1994. The bleaching syndrome: Implications of light skin for Hispanic American assimilation. *Hispanic Journal of Behavioural Sciences,* 16:307-314.

Hall, R.E. 1995. The bleaching syndrome: African American response to cultural domination vis-à-vis skin colour. *Journal of Black Studies* 26:72-184.

Harris, M. 1970. Referential ambiguity in the calculus of the Brazilian racial identity. *Southwestern Journal of Anthropology* 26:1-14.

Hasenbalg, C. A., and N. do V. Silva. 1999. Race and educational opportunity in Brazil. In *Race in Contemporary Brazil: From Indifference to Inequality*, ed. R. Reichmann, 53-66. PA: Pennsylvania State University.

Heinz, A. 1990. *Jewish Immigrants, Mass Consumption and the Search for American Identity.* New York: University of Colombia Press.

Henriques, F. 1953. *Family and Colour in Jamaica.* London: Eyre and Spottiswood.

Hobson, J. 2005. *Venus in the Dark: Blackness and Beauty in Popular Culture.* United Kingdom: Routledge.

Hope, D. 2011. From browning to cake soap: Popular debates on skin bleaching in the Jamaican dancehall. *Journal of Pan-African Studies* 4(4):165-194.

Jarrín, A. 2010. Cosmetic citizenship: Beauty, affect and inequality in southeastern Brazil. PhD thesis, Duke University, USA.

Kymlicka, W. 1995. *Multicultural Citizenship: A Liberal Theory of Minority Rights.* Oxford: Clarendon Press.

Machado-Borges, T. 2008. O antes e depois: Feminilidade, classe e raça na revista plástica e beleza. *Luso Brazilian Review* 45:146-162.

Machado-Borges, T. 2009. Producing beauty in Brazil: Vanity, visibility and social inequality. *Vibrant* 6: 208 -237.

Mandela, N. 1995. *Long Walk to Freedom.* London: Abacus.

Marx, A. 1998. *Making Race and Nation: A Comparison of the United States, South Africa, and Brazil.* Cambridge University Press.

Mbeke, M. 2009. *Architects of Poverty: Why African Capitalism Needs Changing.* South Africa: Pan Macmillan.

McCallum, C. 2005. Racialized bodies, naturalized classes: Moving through the city of Salvador da Bahia. *American Ethnologist* 32:100-117.

McCauley, D. 2010. *Dog-Heart.* United Kingdom: Peepal Tree Press.

McRobbie, A. 2009. *The Aftermath of Feminism: Gender, Culture and Social Change.* Los Angeles and London: Sage Publications Ltd.

Miller, E. 2001. Body image, physical beauty and colour among Jamaican adolescents. In *Caribbean Sociology: Introductory Readings*, ed. R. Reddock and C. Barrow, 305-319. Kingston: Ian Randle Publishers.

Mire, A. 2001. Skin bleaching: poison, beauty, power and politics of the colour line. *Resources for Feminist Research* 28:13-38.

Mohammed, P. 2000. But most of all mi love me browning: The emergence in the eighteenth and nineteenth century Jamaica of the mulatto woman as the desired. *Feminist Review* 65:22-48.

Nutall, S. 2006. Introduction: Re-thinking beauty. In *Beautiful/Ugly: African and Diaspora Aesthetics.* Durham: Duke University Press.

Reichmann, R. 1999. *Race in Contemporary Brazil: From Indifference to Inequality.* PA: The Pennsylvania State University Press.

Ribane, N. 2006. *Beauty... A Black Perspective.* South Africa: University of Kwa-Zulu Natal Press.

Robotham, D. 2000. Blackening the Jamaican nation: The travails of the black bourgeoisie in a globalized world. *Identities: Global Studies in Culture and Power* 7:1-38.

Rodrigues, N. 1977. *Os Africanos no Brasil.* São Paulo: Cia Ed. Nacional.

Sanjek, R. 1971. Brazilian racial terms: Some aspects of meaning and learning. *American Anthropologist* (N.S.) 73:1126-1143.

Sansone, L. 2003. *Blackness without Ethnicity: Constructing Race in Brazil.* New York: Palgrave Macmillan.

Schwarcz, L.M. 1993. *The Spectacle of the Races: Scientists, Institutions, and the Race Question in Brazil 1870-1930.* New York: Hill and Wong.

Shepherd, V., and H. Beckles, eds. 2000. *Caribbean Slavery in the Atlantic World.* Jamaica: Ian Randle Publishers.

Sheriff, R. E. 2001. *Dreaming Equality: Colour, Race and Racism in Urban Brazil.* New Brunswick: Rutgers University Press.

Strasser, S. C. McGovern, and M. Judt.1998. *Getting and Spending.* Cambridge: Cambridge University Press.

Taussig, M. T. 2012. *Beauty and the Beast.* Chicago: University of Chicago Press.

Telles, E. E. 2004. *Race in Another America: The Significance of Skin Colour in Brazil.* Princeton and Oxford: Princeton University Press.

Wagley, C. 1957. Plantation America: A culture sphere. In *Caribbean Studies: A Symposium*, ed. Vera Rubin, 3-13. Seattle: University of Washington Press.

Wolf, N. (1991) *The Beauty Myth: How Images of Beauty are Used Against Women.* New York: William Morrow and Company.

Zelizer, V. (1997) *The Social Meaning of Money.* Princeton: Princeton University Press.

BEYOND THE PALE?

Skinderella Stories and Colourism in India

ANNIE PAUL

Abstract   This article examines the pervasive phenomenon of skin bleaching in India. It highlights the increasing consumption of skin bleaching products by both Indian women and men as an outcome of a deeply embedded practice of colour discrimination in the nation. Notably, the faces that appear on Indian television and the film industry (Bollywood) are almost exclusively fair-skinned. In the marriage trade "fair skin" is virtually the single most highly prized attribute that a bride can command. Consumption of fairness creams and other skin lightening products is boosted by a battalion of television, magazine and social media advertising, using top Bollywood actors.

Although the origin of the dominant beauty ideal of paleness in India is debatable – considering that the ideal of light skin predates colonialism – it is clear that contemporary yearnings for fairer skin are driven by a combination of Western mass-mediated ideologies and traditional Asian cultural values.

Key words • Skin bleaching • Skin lightening products
• Beauty ideal • Bollywood

Representations of skin whitening are strategic and localised and sufficiently generalised to embrace the desires of Asian women and men – some advertising explicitly calls on desire for male approval, and endorses fair skin as something essential to femininity. The advertising specifically resurrects a regime of visible contrast and comparison based on the binaries of both patriarchal as well as colonial hierarchies. The advertisements project an imaginary set of propositions: 'Am I darker or fairer than this model?" "Is my boyfriend staring at that woman who just happens to be paler than me?" "It doesn't matter that my boss prefers my colleague – I'm lighter than her". Worth and cultural capital becomes re-associated with a paleness which makes the subject stand out – in a class- and colonially-positive way – from the rest of the darker ethnic mass (Goon and Craven, 2003).

IDEAZ Vol. 14 • 2016 • ISSN 0799-1401 (133–145)
© Centre for Tourism & Policy Research / Ian Boxill – UWI, Mona

In the 21st century it is becoming apparent that skin lightening practices are something of a global phenomenon. From Kingston to Mumbai to Lagos to Seoul bleaching facial skin using a variety of chemical and natural products is an overwhelming obsession with large numbers of people.[1] What exactly is driving this mania is a question that continues to baffle scholars even as billions of dollars are spent worldwide buying skin their owners can feel comfortable in.

To take bleached countenances at face value would suggest that globally there is a preference for pale, light or white skin and an aversion to darker-complected skin. The Caucasian practice of tanning bodies in the sun or under lamps to temporarily acquire darker skin is an exceptional counter-custom in which brown skin is glossed as fashionable and desirable. There are not many examples of this type of reversal of colour values.

THE CURRENCY OF WHITENESS/LIGHTNESS

Reasons for bleaching one's face vary from location to location depending on the particular historical circumstances involved as well as the interplay between the politics of beauty and colour in that place and global standards of beauty. Although there is a tendency to associabte attempts to lighten skin colour with the after-effects of colonial racism there is plenty of evidence in Asian countries to suggest that the ideal of white or light skin predated colonialism. According to Li et al. (2008):

> 'White skin' has emerged as a central desideratum of consumer culture in affluent Asia. Not only does skin lightness affect perceptions of a woman's beauty, it also affects her marital prospects, job prospects, social status, and earning potential (Ashikari, 2003; Goon and Craven, 2003; Leslie, 2004). The beauty ideal of white skin in Asia predates colonialism and the introduction of Western notions of beauty (e.g., Wagatsuma, 1967). Contemporary meanings of white skin combine Western mass-mediated ideologies and traditional Asian cultural values.

The hegemony of whiteness, its insuperable position at the top of the pyramid, is carefully cultivated and maintained. According to Goon and Craven (2003):

> Lipsitz (1998) coins the phrase the 'possessive investment in whiteness'... to describe how European Americans have used whiteness to create and secure economic advantages, while 'white power secures its dominance by seeming not to be anything in particular'.... Lipsitz's phrase (1998) initiates a metaphor

in which 'whiteness' is currency that exists invisibly, in not seeming to be colour at all, while forcing on 'racialised' groups, competition for white approval – an expense or cost literalised in the purchase of skin-whitening products.

In India colour discrimination probably has deep roots going back to the days when the dark-skinned Dravidians who inhabited North India were driven South by fair-skinned Aryan invaders from Greece and Central Asia. Later the fair-skinned Mughal dynasties held sway and then white-skinned European colonizers. Whatever the history of colour-based discrimination in the subcontinent, the antipathy towards dark skin is overt, even blatant, today and is underpinned by very powerful epidermally marked signification.

Thus in both the Indian television and film industries desirable faces – those of news readers, protagonists of celluloid dramas or tv soap operas and advertising models – are almost exclusively light-skinned. In the marriage trade "fair" skin is virtually the single most highly prized attribute a bride can command. Achieving the desired skin colour and tone is a consideration even in the foetal stage when Indian mothers-to-be are urged to consume white-coloured foods – yoghurt, rice, cashews and almond milkshakes – in an effort to lighten the complexion of their babies. The skin colour aspired to occupies a range and is not fixed to one shade only:

> The normative palette of idealized light skin color in India may be anchored to a flexible and complex process of racial and ethnic coding that fluctuates with a crisscrossing matrix of global influences (travel and media consumption) and local social formations (region, ethnicity, class, family, education, religion). The precise shades of 'fair' skin that Indian women may aspire to possess can thus range from the white skin color associated with Northern European Caucasians to [the] olive skin color associated with Southern European Caucasians and the North Indian Punjabi community (Parameswaran and Cardoza, 2009).

The insatiable demand for fair skin has resulted in traditional skin-lightening practices in India becoming commodified, and a plethora of commercial preparations are now available claiming to render dark skin fashionably pale. The first commercial preparation, Fair and Lovely, appeared in 1978. Until recently skin-lightening creams were aimed mainly at women but in 2005 a fairness cream for men was launched – Fair and Handsome (Fig. 6.1). This cream is reportedly a big hit among men in Southern India where complexions are darker than in the North.

Figure 6.1 • Fair and Handsome Cream

According to Shantanu Guha Ray (2010a):

> A recent study by Hindustan Unilever showed how men in southern states like Tamil Nadu, Kerala, Andhra Pradesh and Karnataka are fervent purchasers of whitening creams. For example, Tamil Nadu has been recording – for the last year – the highest number of sales for Narayanan, a skin-whitening cream from the Unilever stable....

> Asian markets in general have seen a dramatic growth in the turnover of skin whitening and lightening products which are now the best-selling product categories in the Asian beauty industry making up 40 to 50 percent of the cosmetics market in India....

According to the HubPages (2013) Internet article, "Skin Colour Matters – How to Become Fair":

> Companies manufacturing / marketing fairness creams in India are registering a steady growth in their business turnover. The sales of some well-known brands like Fair and Lovely of Hindustan Lever and White Perfect from L'Oréal are reportedly growing by 18% annually. The reputed research agency AC Nielsen has further projected that that the market for fairness cream in India will grow by up to 25% in the current year.

SKINDERELLA STORIES

Consumption of fairness creams and other skin-lightening products is boosted by a battalion of television, magazine and social media advertising using top Bollywood actors such as Aishwarya Rai and Shah Rukh Khan as models. Unilever, one of the largest manufacturers of fairness creams, even employed Facebook to market its products with an application that allowed men to upload photos of themselves, lighten their skin colour and then use the modified images as their Facebook profile photos, much as they promised their new lightening cream would deliver. Bollywood star Shahid Kapur was the face of the campaign (Fig. 6.2).

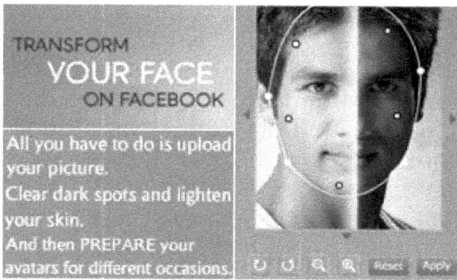

TRANSFORM
YOUR FACE
ON FACEBOOK

All you have to do is upload your picture.
Clear dark spots and lighten your skin.
And then PREPARE your avatars for different occasions.

Figure 6.2 • Unilever Facebook Campaign

A plethora of descriptors is employed to promote the cosmetic processes: "lightening, brightening, clearing, whitening, anti-pigmentation, freshening, anti-dullness and even illuminating" (Shantanu Guha Ray, 2010a). In one instance the product promised to deliver a "pinkish-white glow" with a choice of "pale white" or "pinkish white". Most advertisements show the fortunes of young women, transformed by the skin lightening product in question, displaying a drastic, Cinderella-like upturn. Post-skin lightening, they are revealed attracting the best bridegrooms, jobs and lifestyles. The plugs often show a woman seeking a man's approval after having her skin lightened with the help of the products concerned.

These preposterous fairness narratives are barely credible and are often scoffed at in the public sphere, yet the products continue to sell suggesting that many consumers are suspending their disbelief long enough to buy them. Parameswaran and Cardoza (2009) also discuss the co-option of "the cosmopolitan aura of scientific modernity" in advertising:

> The didactic language, neutral tone and terse pace of ad copy, and the liberal sprinkling of medical jargon in a number of ads immerse fairness products in the smog of scientific authority. Addressing consumers as rational subjects, these discursive advertising tactics affirm the systematic and linear path towards beauty that lies dormant in jars and tubes (Parameswaren and Cardoza, 2009: 247).

It is also noted that domestic brands of fairness cream soon started invoking indigenous scientific traditions against the synthetic blandishments of Western science when foreign creams entered the Indian market. According to Parameswaren and Cardoza (2009: 249):

> The birthing of a new branding strategy based in the national-ist rhetoric of indigenous natural science, an authentic source of ethnic beauty for Indian women, takes place in 2000 when competition in the fairness market intensified and multinationals' whitening cosmetics began to threaten the domination of estab-lished national brands. Emami Corporation was among the first candidates (Cavinkare, Dabur, Ayur, Lotus Herbals, and Hindustan Lever) to launch a campaign of ethnic marketing that promised Indian women a 'natural' alternative to the chemical artifice of Western science.

| ORDINARY CREAMS | FAIR N' LOVELY CREAM | FAIR N' LOVELY CREAM + FACE WASH | FAIR N' LOVELY KIT |

Figure 6.3 • Fair and Lovely

(http://feminspire.com/skin-lightening-racial-identity-and-societal-beauty-standards-stopthe madness/)

The advertising discourse around skin bleaching in India is quite similar to that in other Asian countries. As Goon and Craven (2003) note:

> Advertisements and TV commercials for skin-whitening prod-ucts in Malaysia, for example, generally inscribe their texts with a 'from-ugly-duckling-to-swan' fairy-tale. For instance, 'Blossom Into a Fairer Beauty with Lifecella Whitening Mask' is a promise to transform the user 'into the fair beauty you were meant to

be'. The pleasure promised by the product, as indicated by the advertising discourse, is in the response of those who will see you – that is, in the return of a distinctly colonising, value-inscribed gaze. Whiteness is being sold as a new cosmetic product, an 'effect' you can buy and put on. It is a product which, on the one hand, seems to reduce the original value of whiteness (since everyone can now be 'white'), but on the other, reifies the dichotomy and hierarchy between 'white' and 'not-white', and 'white' and 'black/coloured'.

So profitable is the skin lightening industry in India that innovations such as Clean and Dry, an "intimate wash", crop up from time to time. Appearing in 2012 this product is touted as the ultimate in lightening a woman's "private parts". The television ad shows a middle or upper class couple in their modern apartment. The woman seems unhappy as her husband is engrossed in the morning newspapers and unaware of her while drinking his tea. After a liberal dose of the vaginal wash, the woman reappears in shorts vivaciously frolicking on the furniture and teasing the man who swings her up in his arms, evoking marital bliss.

The tagline of the ad says: "Life for women will now be fresher, cleaner and more importantly fairer and more intimate."

Most ads for skin lightening products portray men and women caught negotiating modern, middle class predicaments of how to visibly signify their status and success in society. According to Parameswaran in an article written by Rosemary Pennington (2009), published on Indiana University's Media School Website:

> India's role on the world stage is changing... It's becoming a bigger player in the global economy, is moving from Third World to First World. And, so, these ads are telling people that they need to become modern, that, in order to become part of 'New India', they need to buy these products. This becomes an issue of social mobility, the idea that if you have lighter skin you are more beautiful, you will be more successful, you will be able to change your place in society more easily.

In the Asian context light skin is more often a signifier of class than race as Balmain (2013) points out, writing about South Korea. She remarks, "A pale skin indicates someone who doesn't have to labour outdoors in the harsh sunlight; someone who can afford to stay indoors all day, cultivating and maintaining the "fair complexion" so highly prized by Indian society.

> To be 'white' is to be privileged and in a position of power as whiteness functions as a marker of social status and deter-

mines one's position in the complex system of hierarchy that is an integral component of South Korea's social order.

DARK IS BEAUTIFUL

In recent years there has been a concerted effort by some interest groups to remedy the unfair situation of colourism in India by starting a Dark is Beautiful campaign. This has been successful enough to force the Advertising Standards Council of India (ASCI) to issue new guidelines for advertisers proscribing the communication of any discrimination or the reinforcement of negative social stereotyping on the basis of skin colour (see Appendix). At the same time in Bollywood, actress Nandita Das is practically a lone voice speaking out against colour discrimination. Das has often faced directors and makeup artists trying to lighten her dusky skin when she plays the role of an educated, upper-class woman. She asserts: "They always say to me, 'Don't worry, we will lighten you; we're really good at it' – as a reassurance. It's perpetuating a stereotype that only fair-skinned women can be educated and successful" (Rajesh, 2013).

Changing such deeply held prejudices and practices will take a long time. The subject of colour had come up in 1947 during the lead-up to independence when India"s leaders were debating the fundamental rights to be included in the charter of rights. Freedom from discrimination against colour was not included in the non-discrimination clauses of the Fundamental Charter of Rights because colour discrimination was not legally sanctioned, therefore it was not justiciable, even though deeply ingrained social prejudice against dark skin was widespread.

H. V. Kamath, a member of India's constituent Assembly had moved for anti-colour discrimination legislation to be included in the charter of rights (Constituent Assembly Debates, 1947):[2]

> As regards 'colour' perhaps it is included in the word 'race'. Yet I have my own doubts on that point as well. Personally, I do not think that the word 'race' should find a place here, as that would mean that we recognise a multiplicity of races in India – a doctrine to which I do not subscribe. Yet if ethnologists who are present here think that there are many races in India and the word 'race' must be there, I will yield to them on that point. But I think in that case the word colour should find a place in this clause.
>
> *An Hon'ble Member*: What do you mean by colour?

Mr. H. V. Kamath: 'Colour' means colour of your complexion. Two persons may belong to the same race but may have different colours physically. Therefore to make it comprehensive I move:

That in sub-clause (1) and (2) of clause 4, after the word 'caste' the words 'colour, creed' be inserted.

However Sardar Vallabhai Patel, who was in charge of the Constituent Assembly's Advisory Committee on fundamental rights disagreed and the matter of colour which had been raised along with "political creed" as candidates for non-discrimination clauses, was dropped once and for all.

Sardar Patel's response was:

The non-discrimination clause is restricted to, or is provided for on grounds of religion, race, caste or sex. He wants 'political creed' also to be included. I think it is an absurd idea to provide for non-discrimination as regards a political creed. Political creed may be of any kind. There may be some political creeds highly objectionable. Some may not be deserving of discrimination, but may actually be deserving of suppression altogether. So, I think it does not fit in here. The other amendment relates to colour. I do not know what is the meaning of it. There are different kinds of colours among Indians themselves. Have we got to provide for all of them? Therefore, I do not think all these amendments are necessary at all (Constituent Assembly Debates, 1947).

The predicament of the dark-skinned Indian is one that is unlikely to be resolved in the near future. Modification – the bleached face – and its commodification by the fairness industry, representing mega profits for a cosmetic-industrial complex, will be virtually impossible to dismantle. There also seems to be widespread consensus In India that dark skin is a liability, in contrast to the social capital of "fair skin", ensuring that colour prejudice is built into the socialization of Indian citizens. There is not a single dark-skinned face to be seen in leading roles in films, television serials, advertisements or news shows. This visual apartheid is reinforced by mythological, literary and other non-visual texts that also exclusively gloss the successful, "good" Indian as being fair-skinned while dark skin connotes inferiority and is reserved for villains, servants, drudges and other "bad" or unworthy Indians.

Moreover very few see anything wrong with the status quo. This is markedly different from a country like Jamaica that also has a problem with skin bleaching. Images of successful dark-skinned people abound – Usain Bolt and the other runners, the singing stars and DJs, are all unequivocally dark-skinned. A few years ago when top DJ Vybz Kartel bleached his face several shades lighter there was a national outcry against it and the subject still rouses the ire of many. Explicit advertising of skin lightening products is non-existent although there are any number of homemade remedies available in addition to the usual commercial preparations.

Yet "the cultural resilience of hierarchies of skin color" in both India and the Caribbean remains the same, behooving us to probe further into what causes people in such divergent cultures to employ techniques of skin lightening and what these de-pigmentation processes mean. How do we read the desire for pale skin? Goon and Craven (2003) have an interesting take on this:

> The white-faced Asian subject is a poacher of these narratives of desire, who reconfigures both past and present understandings. For the poacher, 'whiteness' at once references and destabilises colonial narratives. Whiteness, in this sense, is no longer the exclusive marker of the colonising culture or of the aristocrat – it is packaged in bottles and available at a price (in all senses), and may be bought, sold, rejected or adopted according to choice.

On the other hand Balmain (2013) citing Rey Chow (2010) talks of:

> a lived reality in which the social subject needs to part with aspects of themselves that are not considered socially accept-able, in order to gain acceptance into a particular social group. The prevalence of cosmetic surgery procedures and popularity of skin-whitening products in South Korea, and across other Asian countries, can be read as a signifier of this disavowal of self in order to be accepted into the global cosmopolitan community, in which whiteness remains the invisible signifier of power and privilege.

Which of these readings is true? Are they mutually exclusive? Do they co-exist? These remain questions for further studies and investigations into the phenomenon of skin lightening in the 21st century. This article has merely given an overview of the existing research into the discourse of fairness and light-skin fetishism in India.

APPENDIX
THE ADVERTISING STANDARDS COUNCIL OF INDIA

August 14, 2014

Guidelines of Advertising for Skin Lightening or Fairness Improvement Products

PREAMBLE:

While all Fairness products are licensed for manufacture and sale by relevant state Food & Drug Administrations (FDA) under the Drugs & Cosmetics Act, there is a strong concern in certain sections of society that advertising of fairness products tends to communicate and perpetuate the notion that dark skin is inferior and undesirable. ASCI code's Chapter III.1(b) already states that advertisements should not deride race, caste, colour, creed or nationality. Yet given how widespread the advertising for fairness and skin lightening products is and the concerns of different stakeholders in society, ASCI therefore felt a need to frame specific guidelines for this product category. The following guidelines are to be used when creating and assessing advertisements in this category.

1. Advertising should not communicate any discrimination as a result of skin colour. These ads should not reinforce negative social stereotyping on the basis of skin colour. Specifically, advertising should not directly or implicitly show people with darker skin, in a way which is widely seen as, unattractive, unhappy, depressed or concerned. These ads should not portray people with darker skin in a way which is widely seen as at a disadvantage of any kind, or inferior, or unsuccessful in any aspect of life particularly in relation to being attractive to the opposite sex, matrimony, job placement, promotions and other prospects.

2. In the pre-usage depiction of products, special care should be taken to ensure that the expression of the model/s in the real and graphical representation should not be negative in a way which is widely seen as unattractive, unhappy, depressed or concerned.

3. Advertising should not associate darker or lighter colour skin with any particular socio-economic strata, caste, community, religion, profession or ethnicity.

4. Advertising should not perpetuate gender-based discrimination because of skin colour.

Notes

1   Films such as *Dark Girls*, the 2012 film by American filmmakers Bill Duke and D. Channsin Berry, document the problem of colourism worldwide, and the multi-billion dollar bleaching cream industry generated by the preference for light skin.

2   I'm deeply indebted to Anil Nauriya for our initial discussions on the non-inclusion of colour in India's Charter of Fundamental Rights that eventually led me to this very rich historical record.

References

Ashikari, Mikiko. 2003. Urban middle-class Japanese women and their white faces: Gender, ideology and representa

Chow, Rey. 2010. Seeing modern China: Towards a theory of ethnic spectatorship. In *The Rey Chow Reader*, ed. Paul Bowman, 92-124. New York: Columbia University Press. tion. *Ethos* 31(1):3-37.

Constituent Assembly Debates on 30 April, 1947. 1947. Constituent Assembly of India – Volume III: Interim Report on Fundamental Rights. New Delhi.

Leslie, Depak. 2004. *A Darker Side of Fair*. Watertown. MA: Documentary Educational Resources.

Li, Eric P. H., Min, Hyun Jeong Min, Russell W. Belk, Junko Kimura, and Shalani Bahi. 2008. Skin lightening and beauty in four Asian cultures. In *NA - Advances in Consumer Research*, Volume 35, ed. Angela Y. Lee and Dilip Soman, 444-449. Duluth, MN: Association for Consumer Research.

Lipsitz, George. 1998. *The Possessive Investment in Whiteness: How White People Profit from Racial Politics*. Phialdephia. PA: Temple University Press.

Parameswaran, Radhika. and Kavitha Cardoza. 2009. Melanin on the margins: Advertising and the cultural politics of fair/light/white beauty in Inida. *Journalism & Mass Communication Monographs* 11(3):213-274.

Wagatsuma, Hiroshi. 1967. The social perception of skin colour in Japan. *Daedalus* 96(2):407-443.

The Internet

Balmain, Colette. 2013 (Feb 5). Black skin/ white skin: Whiteness, women and Westernization in contemporary South Korean horror cinema. Academia edu. https://www.academia.edu/2519062/Black_Skin_ White_Skin_whiteness_women_and_westernisation_ in_contem porary_South_Korean_Horror_Cinema

Goon, Patricia, & Craven, Allison. 2003. Whose debt?: Globalization and white-facing in Asia. *Intersections: Gender, History and Culture in the Asian Context* Issue 9: August (http://intersections.anu.edu.au/)

HubPages | Facial Skin Care. 2013. Skin color matters – How to become fair: the Indian obsession with fairness creams. Updated 18 August 2013 (http://hubpages.com/style/Skin-Color-Matters-How-to-Become-Fair-The -Indian-Obsession-with-Fairness-Creams)

Pennington, Rosemary. 2009. New monograph looks at advertising skin lightening products in India. Published on Indiana University's Media School Website (http://journalism.indiana.edu/gen-eral-news/news new-monograph-looks-at-advertising-skin-light-ening -products-in-india/)

Rajesh, Monisha. 2013. India's unfair obsession with lighter skin. *The Guardian*, 14 August (http://www.theguardian.com/world/short-cuts/....14/indias-dark-obsession-fair- skin?CMP = twt_gu

Ray, Shantanu Guha. 2010a. India's unbearable lightness of being. *BBC News*, 23 March (http://newsvote.bbc.co.uk/mpapps/pag-etools/print/news.bbc.co.uk/2/hi/south_asia/ 8546183.stm? ad = 1)

Ray, Shantanu Guha. 2010b. India's obsession with white is big busi-ness. *The Sunday Times*, 28 March (http://www.sundaytimes. lk/100328/International/int_18.html)

NATURAL SELF—IMAGES:

GALLERY SHOWCASING HAIRSTYLES
MODELLED BY BLACK WOMEN

Figure G-3 • Georgia Love

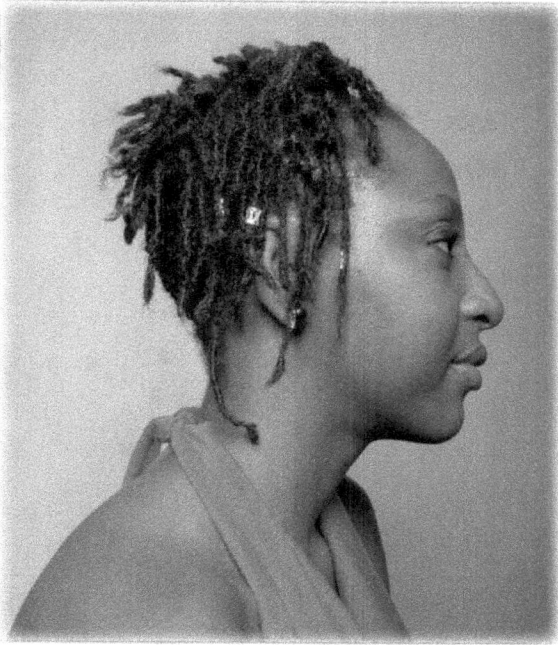

Figure G-4 • Georgia May

Figure G-5 • Flower

Figure G-6 • Danielle McNish

Figure G-7 • Princess Black

NOTES ON CONTRIBUTORS

Michael A. Barnett is Senior Lecturer in Race and Ethnicity, African Diaspora Studies and Social Theory in the Department of Sociology, Psychology and Social Work, The University of West Indies, Mona. His most recent publication "Interrogating Leonard Howell as the First Rasta" appears in *Leonard Howell and the Genesis of Rastafari,* edited by Clinton A. Hutton et al. (2015). He is co-Guest Editor of this issue of *IDEAZ* (v.14, 2016).

Doreen Gordon is Lecturer in Anthropology in the Department of Sociology, Psychology and Social Work, The University of the West Indies, Mona. She specializes in the study of comparative racial formations, religion, social inequality and black cultural forms in Africa and the African Diaspora.

Clinton Hutton lectures in Political Philosophy and Culture at The University of the West Indies, Mona. His latest book is *Colour for Colour Skin for Skin: Marching with the Ancestral Spirits into War Oh at Morant Bay*. Hutton is a noted painter and photographer. He is co-Guest Editor of this issue (*IDEAZ*, v.14, 2016).

Annie Paul is Senior Publications Officer at the Sir Arthur Lewis Institute for Social and Economic Studies (SALISES), The University of the West Indies, Mona. She presently writes a popular blog, "Active Voice", which can be accessed at http://anniepaul.net/

Jean Muteba Rahier is Professor of Anthropology in the Department of Global & Sociocultural Studies at Florida International University where he also serves as Director of the African & African Diaspora Studies Program. He is a renowned anthropologist who is well known for his numerous books on the African Diaspora in Latin America.

Imani M. Tafari-Ama is currently Curator, Flensburger Schifffahrtsmuseum, Flensburg, Germany. A new edition of her highly acclaimed work *Blood, Bullets and Bodies: Sexual Politics Below Jamaica's Poverty Line* (2009) will soon be published.

IDEAZ

Vol 14 • 2016
ISSN 0799–1401

Annual subscription orders:	Individual orders:
• Institutional — US$100 • Individual — US$50	• US$28 • J$3,000

Back issues available online at
www.ideaz-institute.com

Please send subscription & individual orders and enquiries to
email: ian.boxill@uwimona.edu.jm; phone: (876) 970-3931; 970-1467
email: arawakpubl@gmail.com; phone: (876) 758-3373; 822-6705